The Volunteer Tutor's **Toolbox**

Beth Ann Herrmann
University of South Carolina
Editor

Ira

INTERNATIONAL READING ASSOCIATION
Newark, Delaware 19714, USA

The International Reading Association attempts, through its publications, to provide a forum for a wide spectrum of opinions on reading. This policy permits divergent viewpoints without assuming the endorsement of the Association.

Director of Publications Joan M. Irwin
Managing Editor Anne Fullerton
Assistant Editor Amy Trefsger
Editorial Assistant Janet Parrack
Production Department Manager Iona Sauscermen
Graphic Design Coordinator Boni Nash
Design Consultant Larry Husfelt
Desktop Publishing Supervisor Wendy Mazur
Desktop Publishing Anette Schuetz-Ruff
Cheryl Strum
Richard James
Proofing David Roberts

Cover and interior illustrations by Lorraine Sebolt.

Acknowledgments

This book could not have been compiled without the assistance of many people. First, I acknowledge the learners and tutors who worked with the authors and contributors over the years and who inspired us to create this text. Second, the individual authors provided substantive chapters in a timely fashion. Third, I'm grateful to the contributors who were willing to share activities and strategies. Finally, Cindy Grugan provided extraordinary editorial assistance essential for the success of the book.
Beth Ann Herrmann

Editor's Note

Equal contributions were made by authors on coauthored chapters.
BAH

The section "Educational Journals" in Chapter 6 is reprinted by permission of Regie Routman from *Invitations: Changing as Teachers and Learners K-12* (Heinemann, a division of Reed Publishing [USA] Inc., Portsmouth, NH, 1991).

Library of Congress Cataloging in Publication Data

The Volunteer tutor's toolbox / Beth Ann Herrmann, editor.
    p.   cm.
Includes bibliographical references and index.
1. Literacy programs—Handbooks, manuals, etc.   2. Volunteer workers in education—Handbooks, manuals, etc.   3. Reading teachers—Handbooks, manuals, etc.   4. Reading—Handbooks, manuals, etc.   5. Reading (Adult education)—Handbooks, manuals, etc.   6. Tutors and tutoring—Handbooks, manuals, etc. I. Herrmann, Beth Ann.
LC149.V65   1994   93-30992
371.1'4124—dc20   CIP
ISBN 0-87207-394-7

Second Printing, January 1995

Contents

Foreword

I wish I'd had this book in 1960 when I did my first tutoring at the University of Iowa. Now, in my university's second Student Literacy Corps project, I wish my student volunteers had the book. *The Volunteer Tutor's Toolbox* brings together the broad experiences of 11 authors and 7 contributors, over half of whom are themselves Student Literacy Corps trainers. In six chapters practical ideas are shared by these highly educated professionals in such a way as to make the ideas accessible to volunteers who tutor learners of all ages.

Volunteerism has been raised to a high art in the United States. In some other countries, as an IRA colleague remarked to me recently, volunteerism is viewed with a degree of skepticism. Some cannot believe that the altruism of simply helping another could be the central motive of volunteers. On the other hand, the phenomenal growth of volunteerism in the United States has led some to fear that by the end of the century the country will be run mainly by volunteers.

Over the past 30 years major changes have occurred in beliefs regarding the teaching of reading. Words like psycholinguistic, miscue, strategies, holistic, semantic mapping, and integrated learning (wasn't that what Dewey had in mind?), if not entirely unknown in the 1950s, have decided significance in the instructional thinking of today. Fortunately *The Volunteer Tutor's Toolbox* is free of much of the jargon generally found in professional exchanges. Here the presentation of materials is intended for the brand new tutor who may be apprehensive about the first (or even the fourth or fifth) lesson with a young or adult learner.

It is obvious that the writers in this volume favor the current theory of reading known as *whole language.* The role of phonics in reading instruction is almost entirely dismissed. This position may be unpalatable to some already-trained tutors or even to many elementary school teachers. However, the position in this book is much more consonant with current thinking, which sees learners as learning to read and write more readily if a good share of the process comes out of each learner's experiences. Thus, the authors emphasize the language experience approach and individualized reading. In fact, *The Volunteer Tutor's Toolbox* considers student and tutor as necessary partners in the learning process— a process that also promotes the development of decision making. That these learners must become capable decision makers to be included in the democratic processes essential in most of the countries touched by the International Reading Association is but another reason to emphasize that learners are partners, or perhaps even initiators, in their educational experiences.

Volunteerism has emerged as one of the hopes on the adult literacy horizon. With the current awakening to the possibilities of family and intergenerational literacy, volunteers are also being welcomed where doors were once closed—in the elementary and secondary classroom. Volunteers are eagerly offering the individual attention that the busy classroom teacher does not have the time to provide. Here *The Volunteer Tutor's Toolbox* can assist volunteers in answering questions not covered in their initial training. These may include how to determine the characteristics of effective readers, how to make text structure come alive, how to understand effective literacy instruction in general, how to combine reading and writing, or how to assess the progress and success of instruction. A rich collection of resources is provided in this book for answering these and other questions.

As might be expected, some readers may question aspects of the methodology outlined in *The Volunteer Tutor's Toolbox.* Seeking little words in big words, appearing to dismiss phonics instruction, occasionally providing unrealistic suggestions for activities for some age groups, or providing little information about how to record progress are all debatable items. In spite of these points, however, this book offers a quantity of helpful directions for instructing the new reader. In particular, the authors understand how an inexperienced tutor may feel, and they provide practical suggestions to cover a variety of circumstances.

There is an art to identifying those precepts and strategies that will meet the needs of all ages of learners. *The Volunteer Tutor's Toolbox* does this well. The authors have extracted essential tools from the reading workshop and packaged them for use by those who need them most. Some of the rest of us who have had access to the larger workshop will also find them useful.

The larger message in this book may be overlooked if one stands too close to the action. We are witnessing the emergence of thinkers from *all* walks of life. Adult new readers are now participating as leaders in planning meetings for their peers. We have for some time dismissed nonreaders as insignificant players, but let us remember what nonliterate people have contributed—for example, to the founding of the United States. People of courage, energy, and resolve worked their way to the West and are now known as pioneers of new frontiers. Perhaps we are ready to recognize the worth of another whole wave of new readers, people who themselves see their need for next steps in literacy and for others with whom to share the experience. This cherishing of each individual, this recognizing and helping to develop potential, is a possible next step for many. The dedicated volunteer tutor can play an important role in this activity.

Anabel P. Newman
Indiana University

Preface

Congratulations on your decision to become a volunteer literacy tutor. You are joining the efforts of hundreds of individuals all over the world who are dedicated to making a difference in the lives of children and adults who aspire to learn how to read and write.

Having been directors of volunteer literacy tutoring programs or literacy tutors ourselves, we recognized the need for a practical handbook for tutors that provides useful information, tips, and suggestions. That is the purpose of our book. We have taken a broad perspective on literacy tutoring and include here information for working with children, adolescents, and adults in a variety of settings such as schools, adult education programs, churches, prisons, and other community environments.

The book's six chapters are written in a conversational tone for easy reading. Chapter 1 offers practical tips to get you started—developing and maintaining successful relationships, communicating effectively, and planning and implementing lessons. Chapter 2 focuses on effective literacy instruction. Chapter 3 builds on Chapter 2 with information to help you develop a better understanding of what makes effective readers and writers successful. It also includes strategies and activities for tutoring sessions. Chapter 4 includes specific strategies for assisting learners with assigned work.

Chapter 5 focuses on assessment, including many strategies and activities we have used ourselves. Chapter 6 provides recommended resources for additional information and ideas. Finally, Bird B. Stasz provides some provocative final comments about literacy and literacy tutoring to get you thinking beyond your role as a literacy tutor.

We hope this book will not only help get you started with tutoring but also provide you with the impetus and know-how to seek and find additional information from other resources. On behalf of all the authors and contributors, good luck—and don't forget to have fun!

BAH

Authors and Contributors

Authors

Barbara W. Batdorf, reading specialist at Spring Ridge Elementary School in Frederick, Maryland, is the on-site coordinator for FOCUS, a tutoring partnership between Hood College and Spring Ridge Elementary School.

Beverly Griffin Cox is an associate professor in the School of Education at Purdue University in West Lafayette, Indiana, where she teaches graduate and undergraduate courses and conducts research in language and literacy development. She is also the project director for one of the Student Literacy Corps grants based in a collaboration between Purdue University and the Lafayette Adult Reading Academy. Prior to coming to Purdue, Cox taught in the public schools for 12 years and worked as a curriculum developer.

Ellen C. Garfinkel is an assistant professor in the education department at Hood College in Frederick, Maryland, where she teaches both graduate and undergraduate courses, directs the Hood College Summer Reading Clinic, and is codirector for the Student Literacy Corps grant between Hood College and Spring Ridge Elementary School.

Joy Garton Krueger is the director of teacher education and certification at Purdue University in West Lafayette, Indiana, the literacy coordinator at the Lafayette Adult Reading Academy (LARA), and project coordinator for the

Student Literacy Corps grant between Purdue and LARA. Her research interests are in adult literacy, student-teaching preparation, instruction, and materials design. She taught in the public schools for seven years.

Beth Ann Herrmann is an associate professor in the College of Education at the University of South Carolina in Columbia, where she teaches school-based graduate and undergraduate reading methods courses and conducts classroom research with preservice and inservice teachers on literacy teaching and teacher education. She also directs an after-school literacy enrichment program for at-risk students and their parents funded by the U.S. Department of Education Student Literacy Corps Program.

Kathleen A. Hinchman is an assistant professor in the School of Education at Syracuse University in New York. She teaches undergraduate and graduate courses in literacy assessment and instruction and works with several community-based projects to address the literacy needs of adolescents and adults. She just completed a term as codirector of a Student Literacy Corps project at Syracuse University where the opportunity to tutor adults in a variety of settings is now a regular course offered to undergraduate students.

Judy Nichols Mitchell is a professor and chair of the Department of Language, Reading, and Culture in the College of Education at the University of Arizona, Tucson. Her Student Literacy Corps grant focused on the tutoring of at-risk children, youth, and adults in multicultural school settings. Her research interests are in text analysis, reading strategies, and retelling for instruction and assessment of reading comprehension.

Jeri Sarracino is a reading teacher at St. Andrews Middle School in Columbia, South Carolina. Her research interests include cognition and metacognition, whole language, and the restructuring of teacher education.

Bob Schlagal is an associate professor of reading at Appalachian State University in Boone, North Carolina. His scholarly interests include spelling development, early literacy, and the uses of narrative in the classroom. He recently received a National Endowment for the

Humanities grant to study blues music as literature, history, and culture at the Center for the Study of Southern Culture, University of Mississippi.

Jeanne Shay Schumm is an assistant professor in the School of Education at the University of Miami in Coral Gables, Florida, where she teaches graduate and undergraduate courses in literacy. She is director of the university's Student Literacy Corps project, an elementary school–based tutoring program. She is codirector of the University of Miami School-Based Research Project, a research effort focusing on meeting the diverse needs of students in content area classrooms. Schumm has coauthored a textbook for reading resource specialists, a homework book for parents, and a study skills book for middle school students.

Bird B. Stasz is a reading specialist and director of elementary education at Wells College in Aurora, New York, where she teaches courses in reading and writing instruction. She has held faculty positions at the University of Hawaii in Honolulu and Hobart and William Smith Colleges in Geneva, New York. She is also interested in program and material design. She has taught courses and conducted research in the use of oral history, folklore, and folklife in the reading and writing process. She was also a Student Literacy Corps coordinator for Hobart and William Smith Colleges. Stasz has taught in elementary and secondary public schools as well as in adult-education programs. She recently coauthored a textbook on using personal narrative to help adults learn to write.

Contributors of Strategies and Activities

Lilia Dale, El Paso Community College, El Paso, Texas

Altamese Hamilton, Hillsborough Community College, Tampa, Florida

Pam Hudson, Crowder College, Neosho, Missouri

Janet Lambert, Eastern Illinois University, Charleston, Illinois

Sam Mathews, West Florida University, Pensacola, Florida

Kay Taggart, El Paso Community College, El Paso, Texas

Josephine Young, West Florida University, Pensacola, Florida

CHAPTER 1

Practical Tips for Volunteer Tutors

Judy Nichols Mitchell

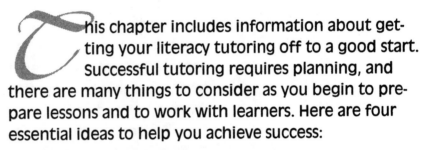

This chapter includes information about getting your literacy tutoring off to a good start. Successful tutoring requires planning, and there are many things to consider as you begin to prepare lessons and to work with learners. Here are four essential ideas to help you achieve success:

1. Know the goals and operating procedures of the literacy program in which you volunteer.
2. Know about the learners who are going to receive your services.
3. Know how to plan appropriate lessons to help learners.
4. Know how to interact with learners to make your lessons run smoothly.

As you prepare yourself in each of these areas, you'll begin to feel more at ease with your tutoring situation. Remember, the more comfortable you are with your literacy program and with your role as a volunteer, the more likely you are to be successful with your tutoring.

Know Your Literacy Program

Most communities offer many types of literacy programs. Basically, these programs can be divided into two groups: those for adults and those for children.

Adult Programs

- ABE
- GED
- English as a second language

Adult programs usually serve learners age 16 and older. Sometimes the learners have completed high school, but, more frequently, they have dropped out of high school for various reasons. The focus of some of these literacy programs is to help learners prepare for their high school equivalency exam. Other programs focus on Adult Basic Education (ABE) or skills below high school level. Although learners below age 22 may be eligible for regular high school services in most U.S. states, many young adult learners prefer to receive services through an adult literacy program because they have not been successful in regular school programs.

Other adult literacy programs in the United States serve needs beyond ABE or GED (General Equivalency Diploma) literacy instruction. Often these programs combine literacy instruction with learning that prepares individuals for trades or occupations. Still other adult literacy programs teach literacy skills to learners for whom English is a second language. These students learn English while learning to read and write. Learners who can already read and write in another language have a strength they can transfer to their study of English: as with many other types of learning, it is easier to transfer and apply knowledge one already has than to acquire new learning. But those who have never learned to read or write in their first language have to build their initial knowledge of literacy as a process in addition to learning English as a second language.

Literacy programs for children are offered through schools, clubs, and neighborhood centers. Some of these programs help children improve basic literacy skills, while others strive to enhance children's literacy through exposure to special topics, materials, and projects. Some after-school programs help learners with school assignments and homework, usually under the direction of a teacher. The type of tutoring involved in these programs is described in Chapter 4.

Literacy programs that serve both adults and children are called family or intergenerational literacy programs. These programs help adults and their children or grandchildren by increasing the literacy levels of everyone in the family. Some family literacy programs focus on teaching adults how to be supportive of their children's learning in schools; other programs provide separate educational experiences for each generation according to its respective needs. Family literacy programs are one way of breaking the cycle of low literacy, school failure, and school drop-out, which seems to recur in some families generation after generation.

The level of responsibility assigned to volunteer tutors may differ according to whether literacy programs serve adults or children. In some programs, teachers prepare instructional plans for tutors to follow; other programs may have a specific curriculum. These types of programs require tutors to do less planning than those in which tutors are expected to create the instructional plans themselves. In either case, training is usually provided for tutors so they can successfully carry out their roles in the tutoring sessions. This book contains many suggestions and ideas for planning and teaching that can be incorporated into actual tutoring.

You may want to ask some questions about your own literacy program: What is the focus of this program? What is the main educational goal for the learners? What kind of records should I keep of my tutoring sessions? How frequently and with whom should I discuss the tutoring sessions and the progress of my learners? What resources and materials are there to help me in my tutoring? To whom should I go if I have a tutoring problem? Answers to these questions will help you become a successful tutor.

Know Your Learners

Most volunteer literacy tutors report that they learn a lot from their learners. In fact, while tutoring, volunteers may learn as much as they teach. Tutoring involves personal contact with one or more learners for an extended period. Like all interpersonal relationships, tutoring is built on mutual trust and respect between the volunteer and the learner.

Tutoring is similar to coaching a sport. Good coaches know a lot about what they teach, but they also know a lot about their athletes. Coaches know what their athletes can do and what they need to learn next. Coaches also know how to motivate their athletes so they will continue to work hard and improve, even when they get discouraged. Athletes need to have confidence in their coaches to do a good job. They also need honest feedback from their coaches about their progress as they continue to learn.

The job of literacy learning is a cognitive task, but it occurs within a social setting where feelings, attitudes, and motivation play a part in learning. As a volunteer literacy tutor you need to learn how to deal with the social aspects as well as with the cognitive content of what is to be taught and learned. To be a successful tutor, you have to become a coach, providing meaningful content, guiding the learning process, and inspiring the confidence and cooperation of your learners.

Getting to Know Your Learners

How can you do this? The best way is to get to know your learners. This means learning about their literacy skills, to be sure, but it also means learning about their interests—getting to know them as people and seeing how literacy fits into their lives. Although this may sound like a monumental task, it can happen quite naturally as you meet regularly with your learners to work on literacy skills. Just as in all social situations, such personal interaction cannot be one-sided. As a tutor, you will also be involved in the learning context, and you need to let your learners get to know you. As you reveal your own interests and acquaint your learners with how literacy fits into your life, you will begin to build the rapport necessary for enhancing your effectiveness as a literacy tutor.

In literacy learning situations, building a personal rapport may sometimes be difficult because of the learners' past experiences. Your learners may have worked with other tutors and teachers over the years, and they may approach working with you in a way that reflects their earlier experiences. If these experiences have been positive, your learners will usually be open to a new learning situation with you. However, if prior relationships have not been positive, it may take a long time to build a level of trust between you and your learners. In such situations, your best approach is to develop relationships slowly over time and to help your learners gradually learn to trust the sincerity of your interest in working with them and the respect you have for them.

One way to build rapport is to plan an opportunity to share interests during each lesson. Sometimes it can be simply the exchange of information about a topic, such as your favorite colors, TV programs, sports teams, and so on. (There are several published interest inventories that get at this type of information. An example of one is included in Chapter 5.) These ideas will also help you incorporate learners' interests into your literacy lessons.

Another successful activity is the "Three Questions" game in which each person asks three questions and then answers three questions. Make sure the questions being asked and answered are not too personal. Handle questions that are too personal by declaring them off limits and allowing your learners to do the same. You may want to use a "Dialogue Journal" to continue to get to know your learners and to provide a framework for the tutoring sessions. Jeanne Shay Schumm, another author included in this book, suggests following these steps. First, explain the purpose of the dialogue journal as follows:

> This spiral notebook is a place for us to talk about books, reading, authors, and writing. In it you can write letters to me, and I'll write letters back to you. In your letters to me, talk about what you've read. Tell me what you thought and felt and why. Tell me what you liked and didn't like and why. Tell me what these books meant and said to you. Ask me questions or for help, and write back to me about my ideas, feelings, and questions. You can also write to me about your thoughts and feelings about the tutoring session. Let me know what you liked and didn't like. That will help me plan for the next session.

Together with your learners, develop a list of rules for writing in the book, and write them at the beginning of the dialogue journal. You should write the first letter as a model for the learners to follow. If learners' first entries are brief, be patient. As they follow your examples, their entries will grow over time. If a learner has limited writing skills, let him or her dictate the entry. After the dictation, read the entry back to the learner. Dialogue journals should emphasize content rather than form. You should try a technique called "modeling" in your own responses, by using correct spelling and grammar that can serve as an example, or model, for your learners to follow. Be sure to phrase your responses in a positive manner and avoid sarcasm. The purpose of the response is to motivate, not condemn. Finally, be persistent. Many learners are not accustomed to communicating through print. Encourage them to keep trying and make it fun!

As you become friends with your learners over time, you won't need to plan such structured activities to learn about one another—sharing will occur naturally. But it is critical to recognize the value of building personal relationships with your learners. Such knowledge helps you select appropriate materials and activities for your learners as well as establish feelings of motivation and success in the tutoring relationship.

Know How to Plan for Tutoring

In some cases, volunteer literacy tutors carry out lessons from a structured program or receive directions from a supervising teacher. For example, you may be given a book of lessons to follow, or a teacher may ask you to work with a learner on writing an essay. In these situations, even though you are not completely responsible for planning the tutoring session, there are lots of choices in making the tutoring time relevant for your learners.

Working with Your Supervisor

Ask the person directing your program how he or she wants you to work with the learners. In a classroom situation, should you circulate and work with those who ask for help, or should you sit in one place and work with those who come to you? Should you work with everyone or only those one or two people in the class who need extra help? Are there specific materials the learners are expected to use? Do the learners know what assignments they are supposed to be doing? What are the regular teacher's practices in working with learners who need help? Should you provide ideas or suggestions for helping the learners, or should you mainly respond to their questions? What are the teacher's expectations for behavior in the tutoring situation and what things can you do to help learners follow those guidelines? Answers to these questions should help you know what is expected of you and give you some guidance on how to work with learners. More information about handling classroom tutoring situations is provided in Chapter 4.

Planning Lessons

If you are responsible for planning the lessons yourself, you will have fewer constraints and more flexibility in the ways you work with learners, but you will also have less guidance and direction. Planning lessons for literacy learning actually involves identifying a basic structure or framework for the lesson and then planning specific activities to fit the time segments within that framework. For example, most literacy lessons are planned around 30-minute or 45-minute lesson times. Although that may seem like a lot of time to fill with learning activities, lessons become easier to plan if you allocate time to specific segments, as follows:

Lesson Framework

	30-minute lesson	45-minute lesson
Opening activity	3 minutes	4 minutes
Instructional goal 1	10 minutes	15 minutes
Instructional goal 2	10 minutes	15 minutes
Reading activity	5 minutes	8 minutes
Closing activity	2 minutes	3 minutes

An opening activity is something you do to start the lesson. It should be something that is accomplished quickly, to help your learners focus their attention and get ready to work. In your first few sessions, this might be the place for your getting acquainted activities. Later, you can use this time for your learners to engage in brief writing assignments while you get materials organized for the later activities. Your learners' performance during this opening time can give you insight about their literacy strengths or weaknesses, which you can use as a bridge to further learning.

Instructional Goals

The two instructional goals are your main lesson components. Activities during these times should be focused around your learners' instructional needs. Usually one of these goals deals with developing reading comprehension and the other with writing. The particular activities you present during these times may be suggested by the learners' regular teachers, the director of your literacy program, a lesson in an instructional book furnished by your literacy project, or the learners themselves. For example, suppose one of your instructional goals is to help your learners improve their abilities to construct meaning from what they read. During this time in the lesson, you might ask learners to read a short passage on an interesting topic and answer a few questions you have prepared in advance. Or you could ask your learners to tell or write about what they have read. As an alternate activity you could have learners arrange sentences from the passage in sequential order. You will find many more ideas for specific learning activities in Chapter 3.

The important thing to remember about planning or selecting learning activities for the instructional goals components of your literacy lessons is that the activities should be planned according to your learners' needs. The activities should also be short enough to be accomplished within 10- or 15-minute intervals. By completing several small activities within the same lesson, learners gain a sense of accomplishment and success—both of which contribute to maintaining or increasing motivation for learning.

The fourth part of the lesson framework is a brief period of reading, during which your learners can practice what they have learned. This is an important time, because if learners experience success during this part of the lesson, they are more likely to want to read on their own time. Make sure you are available to offer support in case your learners need help.

If your learners are already readers, have them read something of interest to them during this time.

Perhaps they will read their own book for a brief period each lesson, or maybe they will practice with something you used in an earlier lesson. Offer your learners opportunities to read silently, and let them know that you will help them if they get stuck or if they don't understand. After reading silently, learners may want to share some of what they read by reading it aloud to you. Make sure the learners have opportunities to read silently before asking them to read out loud. Often learners think they should always read out loud because that is how previous literacy lessons have been handled. However, it's important for them to read silently first to improve their reading comprehension.

If your learners are not already readers, this is the time in the lesson when you can read to them. Sit beside them so they can follow what you are reading. As learners gain proficiency, they can read with you, or each of you can take turns reading. Make sure you select something of interest to your learners for this part of the lesson. Also, you should recognize that many learners like to hear or read the same text several times for practice.

The final part of the lesson is the closing activity. At this time you should provide your learners with opportunities to think about the lesson, about what they've learned, and about the progress they're making. For example, ask learners to write some brief comments in a journal about what they have learned that day or what they feel good about learning. If it is difficult for some learners to write, you can discuss these points with them and record comments as they dictate.

Some tutors award points for completing each of the lesson activities. During the closing activity, the points can be added up and recorded in a book so learners can see progress. Keep in mind, however, that point systems don't work for everybody. The important thing about the closing activity is for learners to feel a sense of accomplishment at the end of every lesson. That way, they will feel better about participating in the next tutoring session.

These ideas on lesson planning are intended just to get you started. Modify my suggestions according to the needs of your own learners. Other factors to consider in planning are your learners' ages, reading abilities, attention spans, motivation, and the context or environment of your lessons. In general, it is better to plan short activities. If an activity is successful, you can do another similar activity the next time and build on that knowledge. However, if an activity is not successful, you can move on to one which offers greater opportunity for success. In addition, completing several activities within the same lesson contributes to your learners' sense of accomplishment. Completing three short activities makes learners feel more successful than completing one long activity, even though the lesson times might be equivalent.

Know How to Interact with Learners

Remember that when you are tutoring you are building relationships with your learners. You need to communicate and listen carefully in order to help your learners achieve success. Here are some hints for establishing that rapport.

Establish Trust and Respect

Get to know your learners, and let them get to know you. As you work together on literacy skills, you will need to trust and respect one another. Trust is built on mutual respect and friendship, so don't be afraid to spend a little time establishing friendly working relationships, particularly at the early stages of your tutoring.

Don't Talk Too Much

Almost all tutors (like almost all teachers) tend to talk too much in the tutoring or teaching situation. In trying to be helpful and teach learners what they need to know, tutors tend to overexplain, giving more information than is actually needed and often spending precious time on things learners already know. For the most part, learners are accustomed to this situation, because almost all of their previous teachers have done the same thing. Besides, for the learners, it takes less effort to listen than to really contribute to the discussion. They can "tune out" when things get boring or reply in monosyllables. Unfortunately, such minimal response from the learners only encourages tutors and teachers to give more elaborate explanations.

The trick here is to engage learners in true discussion. It's easier than it may seem, particularly in a one-on-one tutoring situation. You need to remember three rules to get your learners talking:

1. Don't explain anything you don't have to explain. Find out what your learners need to know about a problem or question before launching into an explanation.
2. Ask questions your learners can answer. For the most part, this means asking questions about the learners' thinking and their approaches to problem-solving, such as "What do you know about solar energy that would help you answer this question?" or "What do you think this problem wants you to do?"
3. Make sure you allow enough "wait time" for your learners to think through the questions you are asking. Most tutors and teachers don't wait very long after they ask a question, and when they don't get an answer immediately, they either simplify the question or ask it again in different words. Sometimes they even answer the question themselves. Unfortunately, most learners know this, so they just wait for answers to be given to them. Waiting time helps encourage learners to participate in the discussion.

Help Learners Think Independently

A frequent temptation for tutors is to help learners by answering all their questions immediately. However, this does not result in independent learning, since learners must then always rely on having someone at hand to answer their questions rather than on their own thinking. Often learners who have not been successful in school have not had much practice in figuring things out for themselves. To support your learners in developing this type of thinking, try not to answer their questions too quickly. Instead, try to get them to reveal their thinking and reasoning processes. Ask them what they already know about the question or problem you are discussing. In listening to their logic, you can often identify the specific information they need to answer the question at hand without providing too much detail or repeating information they may already know.

Your learners will probably be unfamiliar with this type of discussion. They might become irritated with you or think you are uncooperative because you are not following typical teaching-learning conversational patterns. You may need to explain that you are trying to help them think through the questions and problems so that they can find their own answers.

Encourage Discussion

Encourage your learners to talk about the question, problem, or task at hand. This gives them opportunities to practice using the terms of the academic discipline and the language of reasoning to attack a problem. Learners who have not been successful in earlier learning situations may not have had the opportunity to practice using academic language skills. Verbal rehearsal is one of the most powerful learning tools. Also, in listening to your learners talk about their learning, you will gain information about them, their knowledge base, and their ways of approaching problems. This information will be invaluable to you later as you plan further learning experiences.

Focus on the Learning Processes

Give your learners opportunities to use the information they already have to guess or predict answers to questions or problems. When learners have opportunities to explain what the answers might be or how to go about solving problems, they can focus their attention on the process of learning rather than on the answers to questions or problems. Remember, however, that predicting is a risk-taking activity—one in which your learners may not have had much practice. Learners who have been unsuccessful in school or in other learning situations are usually poor risk-takers; yet the ability to take risks and make predictions is necessary to increase literacy skills. Often learners in literacy tutoring situations have not previously experienced risk-taking in a supportive environment. If you have established a trusting, respectful relationship, you may be able to help your learners begin to take risks, particularly if you listen to their logic and give positive feedback.

Be Honest and Supportive

Give good, honest feedback to your learners' attempts to answer questions or solve problems. If an answer or reasoning is correct, tell your learners in ways that are appropriate for their ages and experience. If an answer is not correct, say it was a good try (if it was), that it was almost right (if it was), or that it was on the right track (if it was). Then give more information for learners to use to answer the question or problem correctly. If you do not provide honest feedback, your learners will not be encouraged or motivated to reveal their thinking the next time. If you create a climate of support, your learners will believe that you will help them by letting them know when they are correct or not correct in their thinking. Gradually, as your learners become more successful, they will become more confident in their own thinking and less reliant on you as a tutor. However, to do this, they need honest (but kind) feedback from you.

Capitalize on Your Learners' Interests

Tailor some parts of your literacy lessons to those areas in which learners have expressed interest. Interest in the topic studied increases learners' motivation to engage in the tasks at hand. In this way, literacy learning is kind of like eating: we always enjoy eating our favorite foods—not just the things that are good for us.

There's an added benefit to working in an area of interest for learners: often it puts learners in a situation of knowing more about a topic than the tutor. You may not be terribly interested in heavy metal music, gardening, or baseball, but this reversal in the teaching-learning relationship almost always promotes honest discussion and real conversational turn-taking between tutor and learners. Observing your learners as they work in a familiar topic area of interest also gives you insight into their literacy strategies. This information can be helpful in other lessons in other topic areas, when you can remind the learners how they handled information successfully when they knew a lot about the topic.

Enjoy Your Tutoring Times

Finally, don't be afraid to have fun in your sessions with learners. Literacy learning is work, but both literacy and learning can be fun too. Help your learners see the fun part by sharing a joke or cartoon or something funny you have clipped from the newspaper that you thought your learners might enjoy.

A Final Word

Trust your ideas and those of your learners as you structure lessons. It's important to choose appropriate materials and appropriate tasks for your learners' needs. And if you involve your learners in some parts of the planning, chances are they will be more interested and motivated, both of which should contribute to their success. And remember to provide a reading time to give your learners opportunities to apply their learning. In a short time, you'll settle into a lesson routine which will make things comfortable for both you and your learners.

CHAPTER 2

Effective Literacy Instruction

Beverly Griffin Cox
Joy Garton Krueger

*I*n this chapter we explain the benefits of using a holistic approach for helping literacy learners of diverse cultures and ages become better readers and writers. Our use of *holistic* emphasizes that speaking, listening, reading, and writing are interdependent parts of the language-development process and that language development is closely related to knowledge, thinking patterns, attitudes, values, and goals.

In the first section of this chapter we address four important issues associated with understanding language and literacy development:

1. What is language?

2. How do language and literacy develop?

3. What do literacy learners have to figure out about written language? and

4. What do literacy tutors need to do to help learners become successful readers and writers?

In the second section we discuss developing positive attitudes and helping literacy learners understand how reading and writing work.

Understanding Language and Literacy Development

What Is Language?

Holistic approach: A means of teaching that emphasizes the whole process rather than isolated parts.

When people are asked, "What is language?" or "What is the purpose of language?" the typical response is that it is a tool for communication. This is the most obvious part of the answer, but there is more to it than this. Language is a human resource that individuals use to organize and interpret their experiences. Language also reflects our social traditions and plays a major role in cognitive development.

How Do Language and Literacy Develop?

If language forms the building blocks for thinking and shapes our view of the world, then it cannot be thought of simply as sounds learned through environmental conditioning and imitation. Rather, language develops from our need to achieve specific results as we interact with others. For example, people need language to interact socially, to inform others, to regulate behavior, to entertain, to explore, and to accomplish goals.

Children who have had rich preschool literacy experiences tend to have an easier time with literacy learning in school. For instance, many young children learn about literacy by watching, imitating, and interacting orally with adults who are engaged in writing a grocery list, jotting a note, or filling out a form. They especially learn by hearing a favorite storybook read aloud, answering questions about the story posed by an adult, or chiming in during reading. Children who have storybook experiences, in particular, develop an impressive array of knowledge about reading, writing, and written language long before they enter school or have any formal literacy instruction. However, appropriate preschool literacy experiences do not directly *teach* particular reading and writing skills. Instead, informal and child-centered experiences and activities in school provide children opportunities to learn those skills by using written language for real purposes to satisfy real needs, such as entertainment, informing others, regulating a situation, or achieving a goal. Within that context, children can be free to interact socially and to experiment and explore whatever uses of print interest them. Such literacy experiences are holistic in that they integrate oral language and written language; they also allow for personal choice and real uses for speaking, listening, reading, and writing.

There is good reason to believe that holistic literacy experiences based on real-world activities can help both elementary children (e.g., Holdaway, 1979) and older learners (Mikulecky & Drew, 1991) become successful readers and writers. For example, the Language Experience Approach (adapted from Stauffer, 1970) promotes real uses for languages by combining oral and written language with individual interests. Kay Taggart and Lilia Dale of El Paso Community College in El Paso, Texas, describe this approach as follows:

Language Experience Approach

Procedure:

1. Ask learners to dictate their thoughts about an experience.
2. Write what the learners say; some learners may prefer to write on their own.
3. Ask the learners to read their "stories."
4. Learners should select words from their stories that they recognize on sight or would like to learn.
5. Write these words on index cards for the learners to review.
6. Use cardboard or posterboard to make a book of short stories written by the learners.

Many years of research support the idea that literacy develops as needed at any age to serve authentic functions. However, we offer a bit of caution here against viewing this insight as a panacea. There may be physical or other problems that can alter this equation for some people. However, for many learners the critical ingredients for literacy development are appropriate experiences with appropriate materials for real purposes.

What Has to Be Figured Out about Written Language?

Clearly oral and written language support each other. However, there are distinctive characteristics of written language that must be learned because written language is not just oral language written down. One obvious way that written language is different is that it uses print. In addition, written language uses certain conventions to address different audiences (Chafe & Danielewicz, 1987). For example, in a lecture a speaker may use words that are easily interpreted or may use the physical situation (for example, by pointing) to aid interpretation. Some written texts, such as a note to a close friend, may also use the situation or shared knowledge as the resource for interpretation (for example, knowing that "she" in the note refers to a certain friend). In these situations, the words carry part of the meaning, but interpretation of the message relies greatly on things or people in the situation and on shared prior knowledge. However, other written texts require readers to use prior knowledge and also to attend to the author's precise words to construct meaning. One way the language of most books differs from common oral language is that the words *are* the author's message rather than being secondary to the message.

Some very young children intuitively understand this difference, while some adults who have literacy problems do not. Following are three texts that display their authors' understanding of this difference between oral and "book" language. The first two were composed by Shirley, a five-year-old who had no formal reading instruction and was not yet attending kindergarten or reading conventionally. Shirley's first story was shared orally with an adult; the second is a version of the same story dictated by Shirley specifically for other children to read. Notice the changes she makes. Her second text is much more selective, organized, precise, and consequently more clearly interpretable for a reader. The third story was composed by Brett, a middle-aged adult with literacy problems. Brett dropped out of school in the tenth grade. At the time he composed his text, he was reading at an elementary level and was attending a community literacy center. Similar to Shirley, Brett had discussed his trip to Hawaii with his literacy tutor. Subsequently, the tutor asked him to write (although he chose to dictate) his story for other learners to read. Notice that Brett does not recognize the need to switch to a more precise way of expressing his ideas for the new audience. He does not seem familiar with either how a future reader will interact with the text or where the reader must attend to get its meaning. Rather than switching to a new set of conventions, Brett maintains conventions that are quite typical and appropriate in a conversation but not in a text to be read by a range of other people. It is clear that Shirley intuitively under-stands different audiences' expectations for focused and organized structure and the placement of precise words within the text, while Brett does not.

Shirley's Oral Story

Well, first we put on our [roller] skates and then some-times we go on the hard floor. And the owner explains the rules. Rule one was not smoking, no gum, no picking up kids. And I think that's all I remember about the rules. And they played a song. And then they played another song, which me and Jennifer did not win so we had to go out off the hard floor until the song was over but we came back on and I never stopped skating in Skate Away....

Shirley's Dictated Story

Once upon a time I went to Skate Away with my mother. And my mom and my dad was supposed to meet us there. Then I met Jennifer (while) putting on my skates. And I went on the hard floor. I skated and skated and skated. I played a few games and skated to the music. It was finally the last song and we went home and went to bed.

Brett's Dictated Story

I got on a plane in Memphis. Then we flew over to California, changed planes which we had an hour layover. From there, we went over and landed at the big island. When we got off, we went to see if we could rent a car, which we did for the days that we spent there. Then we picked up our luggage, loaded it up in our car, and dropped it off at our hotel. We went to get something to eat. So we rested up that evening in the motel. The next morning, we drove around island and looked around a couple of days. We seen brother's house and seen where he had banana trees. Took a plane to the other islands to look around...took a plane back to the big island. We caught a show....

It is critical for literacy learners to recognize the structural differences concerning selectivity, organization, and the placement of precise words in written text. This recognition must be learned in the same way as other aspects of language—through appropriate experiences with appropriate materials. The importance of this literacy knowledge is more obvious for the writer: common sense indicates that a writer must ensure that his or her text is comprehensible to the intended audience. Successful readers, on the other hand, learn to attend to and use these different conventions to interpret writers' meanings.

As a literacy tutor, you should include experiences with diverse text types and uses of language in your lessons. You may also need to help learners become aware of the range of structural differences in texts and the strategies for recalling and comprehending by modeling or through discussion.

Fostering Literacy

Many benefits result from creating a learning environment rich in meaningful social interactions and opportunities to interact with a wide variety of literacy materials. One is that learners will develop more positive attitudes about themselves and about reading and writing. A second is that they will gain knowledge of how reading and writing work.

Helping Literacy Learners Develop Positive Attitudes

Positive attitudes toward self and reading and writing are usually associated with pleasant experiences and successful performances. Readers develop these positive attitudes when they perceive literacy as useful—a resource that helps them understand the world and get things done. Thus, regardless of your learners' ages, the learning environment should be designed to emphasize literacy as serving a purpose. The things that are to be done through literacy should be decided by your learners—at least in part. To promote positive attitudes about literacy learning, it is essential that your learners view the activities and experiences as serving a real, personal need. At the same time, you should be sure that literacy experiences and associated materials are interesting, age-appropriate, manageable, and challenging.

For young children (preschoolers to primary grades), developing positive attitudes about themselves and literacy is relatively straightforward. Through the early elementary years, most children find storybook read-alouds serve a very real purpose—enjoyment. These young learners also enjoy being invited to chime in, make predictions, or otherwise interact with text. Most enjoy writing or dictating activities, exploring writing systems, or composing personal experience or other stories. In general, young children tend to respond eagerly to opportunities to choose and participate in literacy tasks and to practice literacy for many uses (Holdaway, 1979). Given the opportunity and materials, young children will choose to use literacy in many ways, such as writing notes to inform others, pretending to read a prescription in a drugstore play center, making a sign to regulate behavior at the fish tank, or listening to a book about snakes. Primary grade children also respond well to opportunities to select their own reading materials and collaborate with peers at reading and writing tasks. Most look forward to being readers and writers and willingly try the meaningful activities adults offer. In your tutoring sessions you will probably observe significant literacy growth, as well as growth in positive attitudes, simply by supplying one-on-one social and functional language and literacy interactions that may not have been available at home or school. The specific instructional strategies described in this book will help you further that growth.

Most older children, adolescents, and adults who have experienced literacy failure in the early elementary years develop negative attitudes toward themselves, literacy, and school. They also develop theories about what went wrong and coping strategies that may cover the real problem. Turning this attitude around is the first and most challenging task you will face as a literacy tutor. Without positive attitudes toward self and literacy, little learning will be accomplished. A second challenge may be to convince older learners to try new, more meaning-based approaches.

One technique that especially complements the idea that language and literacy are learned as needed is called *individualized learning*. In this approach the learner has some personal control over his or her learning through goal-setting and selection of topics, materials, or activities. This approach has proven successful with learners of all ages—those who achieve well in school and those who do not.

Many adolescents express the feeling that reading and writing are of no use to them. This offers an extra challenge. As a tutor, you need to find ways to demonstrate the usefulness of reading and writing by creating a real need for literacy through other interests and goals. The function of language as entertainment should not be overlooked with adolescents—and even with adults. For example, one particularly hostile adolescent with whom we worked stated adamantly that reading was useless and literacy was certainly not one of his goals. His tutor discovered that he enjoyed the traditional stories of his Native American heritage. Reading myths together became the pathway through which the tutor changed this learner's negative attitude toward reading and writing.

Adults who return for literacy instruction have generally recognized the importance and value of literacy. This recognition of the real-world costs of literacy problems is a major difference between adolescents and adults—and a boon for the adult literacy tutor. However, adults often have negative feelings about their potential as literacy learners. These feelings often are quite reasonably related to a long history of failure. Adult learners may feel incapable or fearful of setting goals or may set unreasonable ones. On the other hand, some adult literacy learners have focused and practical reasons for learning to read. For example, they may want to

Cox & Krueger

learn to read and write to obtain a driver's license, to be promoted at work, or to help a child with homework.

As a literacy tutor you should recognize that adults are especially serious about gaining access to literacy, and they appreciate the collaboration and respect that go with helping design and implement their own literacy learning. You should also recognize that adults bring a wide array of experiences to the task. For example, researchers report that middle-aged people grow increasingly reflective and are able to think about their own theories and thinking processes in ways far beyond what can be expected from a younger learner (Moshman, 1979). Though the need to develop positive attitudes suggests that all learners should be given some control over their literacy learning, adults have particular assets that make the individualized learning approach easier to implement.

In Chapter 5 you will learn about portfolios. A portfolio contains a collection of a student's work that describes growth in literacy learning. Portfolios are a particularly useful tool in building and maintaining positive attitudes across age groups. Young children and adults feel pride in their written products and enjoy sharing them with family and others. In addition, feelings of despair or frustration are often thwarted when learners can review their work and observe their own growth.

Helping Learners Understand How Reading and Writing Work

One of the best ways to learn about how reading and writing work is to become actively, reflectively, and collaboratively engaged with literacy materials for a real and valuable purpose. In your role as a knowledgeable collaborator you must not only model the expert strategic reasoning that goes on when you read and write, but also encourage and offer your learners opportunities to explore, experiment with, and internalize strategic reasoning. In addition, you should provide extensive social and verbal interaction that takes learners to higher levels of thinking and planning.

One way to accomplish this is through direct instruction (Rosenshine & Stevens, 1984). When using direct instruction, you plan what will be done, state what you are doing and why, and explain your thinking and reasoning processes. Learners can practice this type of strategic reasoning with your assistance. The various levels and types of assistance, whether conducted through direct instruction or otherwise, are usually called scaffolding because they provide steps to learning that can be "torn down" or removed as the literacy learner becomes more expert in strategic reasoning. Provide just enough assistance to help your learners do what they cannot do alone. Strive to achieve a balance between challenge and support through your responses to the learner.

Your role in this instructional approach involves two types of modeling that lead learners to a slightly more advanced level. First, you can use mental modeling (Duffy, Roehler, & Herrmann, 1988) to put into words what goes on in your own strategic reasoning processes. By doing so, you provide students with a model they can follow to develop their own reasoning processes. Procedures for a mental modeling technique follow.

Mental Modeling

Procedure:

1. Explain that reading and writing are complex processes that involve thinking and reasoning. Explain that you will be "thinking aloud" as you read or write to illustrate this complexity.
2. Read a short passage out loud. As you read, verbalize the thinking you are doing to construct meaning from the passage and resolve comprehension difficulties.
3. Ask your learners to explore their own thinking and reasoning processes in the same way.
4. Use the same procedure to illustrate thinking and reasoning associated with successful writing.

Second, you can use implicit modeling to demonstrate thinking and reasoning without announcing what you are doing and why. For example, you can prompt an effective strategy for determining the meaning of an unknown word by suggesting that the learner reread or read on to figure out the word. Or you can model higher level thinking by responding to learners' input with questions that move their thinking to a higher plane. In this framework, modeling or other interactions are employed as needed to achieve the reading or writing purpose. Over time we have observed that learners of all ages tend to emulate what they perceive as successful strategic thinking patterns used by the tutor. The thing to remember is that the goals of modeling and of instructional conversation are to help the literacy learner understand how reading and writing work. More detailed information on teaching strategic reasoning follows in Chapter 3.

One last note about helping literacy learners understand how reading, in particular, works. Certainly, reading does require fundamental knowledge about the most consistent letter-sound relationships, and some research attests to the importance of this knowledge of phonics in beginning reading (Adams, 1990). While some people put great faith in the power of phonics, overemphasis on this one cueing system at the expense of others can lead to reading problems (Goodman, 1973), particularly in comprehension and attitude. Real-world reading and writing experiences and materials demand simultaneous interpretation of phonics, semantics, and syntax.

Phonics:
The identification of words by their sounds.

Semantics:
The identification of words by the meaning of the text.

Syntax:
The order of the words in a sentence.

A Final Word

Many adults automatically assign their reading failure to an inability to learn how to "sound out" words. It is important to push these learners beyond sounding out words to begin to treat language as a system for making meaning, but the typical real-world–type exercises and activities recommended for elementary children tend to be rejected by our adult learners. This is a special problem we have found particularly true of many adult literacy learners and one to which we have not found a workable answer. It is a problem adult literacy tutors should be aware of because it has an impact on motivation as well as on literacy development.

References

Adams, M.J. (1990). *Beginning to read: Thinking and learning about print; A summary.* Prepared by S.A. Stahl, J. Osborn, & F. Lehr. Urbana, IL: University of Illinois, Center for the Study of Reading.

Chafe, W., & Danielewicz, J. (1987). Properties of spoken and written language. In R. Horowitz & S.J. Samuels (Eds.), *Comprehending oral and written language* (pp. 83-113). Orlando, FL: Academic.

Duffy, G.G., Roehler, L.R., & Herrmann, B.A. (1988). Modeling mental processes helps poor readers become strategic readers. *The Reading Teacher, 42,* 762-767.

Goodman, K.S. (1973). The 13th easy way to make learning to read difficult: A reaction to Gleitman and Rozin. *Reading Research Quarterly, 8,* 484-493.

Holdaway, D. (1979). *The foundations of literacy.* Sydney, Australia: Ashton Scholastic.

Mikulecky, L., & Drew, R. (1991). Basic literacy skills in the workplace. In R. Barr, M.L. Kamil, P. Mosenthal, & P.D. Pearson (Eds.), *Handbook of reading research: Volume II* (pp. 669-689). White Plains, NY: Longman.

Moshman, D. (1979). To really get ahead, get a metatheory. In D. Kuhn (Ed.), *Intellectual development beyond childhood.* San Francisco, CA: Jossey-Bass.

Rosenshine, B., & Stevens, R. (1984). Classroom instruction in reading. In P.D. Pearson (Ed.), *Handbook of reading research* (pp. 745-798). White Plains, NY: Longman.

Stauffer, R.G. (1970). *The language experience approach to the teaching of reading.* New York: HarperCollins.

CHAPTER 3

Building Characteristics of Successful Readers and Writers

Beth Ann Herrmann
Ellen C. Garfinkel
Barbara W. Batdorf

Why do some people become successful readers and writers while others do not? This is an important question to consider now that you have decided to become a literacy tutor. You can develop a better understanding of your learners' literacy needs—and how to plan instruction to meet those needs—by becoming familiar with the characteristics of successful readers and writers.

This chapter describes three qualities readers and writers need for success: (1) a positive attitude toward self and reading and writing, (2) the ability to comprehend text and create text that can be understood, and (3) the ability to understand how reading and writing work. You can probably think of other characteristics as you contemplate your own literacy abilities, but these three are considered powerful prerequisites to successful reading and writing (Duffy & Roehler, 1989). To build on these points as discussed here and in Chapter 2, instructional strategies and activities are included to help you develop these characteristics in your learners.

As you read each section, think about the learners you tutor or are about to tutor. Ask yourself these questions: How do my learners feel about reading and writing? Why do they feel this way? How well do my learners understand what they read, and how well can they write text that can be understood by others? How well do my learners understand how reading and writing work?

A Positive Attitude

As discussed in Chapter 2, a person's attitude plays a major role in learning to read and write. Successful readers and writers generally have positive attitudes toward themselves and reading and writing. That means they recognize the many uses of reading and writing and appreciate the value of these activities in everyday life. They know that reading and writing are useful tools for meeting real-life needs and goals. Successful readers and writers generally are excited about reading and writing. They experience a sense of satisfaction when they read and write for practical purposes or for enjoyment. For example, when an apartment tenant writes a letter to her landlord about a leaky roof and it is repaired quickly, she feels a sense of pride in her ability to solve problems. Likewise, when a father reads a bedtime story to his young daughter, he feels pride in his ability to open the door to a magical world for someone he loves.

You can help your learners understand the value of reading and writing by reinforcing three fundamental concepts. First, learners need to know that reading is a way to receive a message and writing is a way to send a message. For example, when a person reads a letter from a friend, a message is received. When the person writes a letter back to that friend, a message is sent.

Second, reading and writing can be used strictly for enjoyment or to accomplish desired goals. For example, when a person copies a new recipe out of the newspaper, reading and writing are being used for enjoyment. On the other hand, when a person writes a note to a landlord complaining about the rent, writing is being used to convey an important message and to urge the landlord to take action.

Third, reading and writing are effective ways to gather information and clarify or acquire knowledge.

For example, when a person sits down to read a newspaper article about Russia, new knowledge may be acquired or a misunderstanding may be cleared up. Likewise, when a person writes a letter to the editor of a newspaper, information is being collected and shared to expand someone else's knowledge or to clarify a misunderstanding.

In sum, successful readers and writers understand a fundamental principle underlying reading and writing: what can be said can be written, what can be written can be read, what can be read can be understood, and what can be understood can change the way someone thinks or feels. Understanding these basic tenets can make learning to read and write a much easier task.

Ability to Comprehend and Create Text

Successful readers and writers are able to understand written messages, and they can create cohesive text that others can read and understand. Both of these tasks require effective use of prior knowledge, knowledge about text structure, and the ability to set purposes for reading and writing.

Prior Knowledge

Prior knowledge refers to knowledge accumulated through previous experiences. A person's ability to understand and create text that can be easily understood by others depends on his or her prior knowledge about a specific topic and how effectively that knowledge is used. For example, a person who knows a lot about flying airplanes is probably familiar with the meanings of technical terms associated with this activity. When this knowledge is used to understand a magazine article about how to make a good landing, new information may be acquired. When the knowledge is used to write in a personal diary about a particularly successful landing, a meaningful message can be shared. On the other hand, if the person does not know much about flying airplanes, he or she would have a difficult time constructing meaning from text containing technical language, and it would also be difficult to write a cohesive paragraph about making a good landing.

You can help your readers learn how to activate and use their prior knowledge to construct meaning from text by trying the K-W-L approach (Ogle, 1986). This strategy will help children or adults interpret what they read using a simple three-step process: drawing on what they *know*, deciding what they *want* to know, and recalling what they *learned* by reading the passage. To use this approach in an individual or group setting, you'll need a section of text and a blank K-W-L chart. A sample chart for the topic "cats" is shown below.

K-W-L Chart for the Topic "Cats"

K—What I *know*	W—What I *want* to *know*	L—What I *learned* or still need to learn
• house pets • drink milk • playful • Siamese	• care of • why they shed • different types	

The first step of the procedure is to help learners brainstorm what they already know about a selected topic. Be sure to choose a topic specific to the text. Then ask learners to write what they already know about the topic on a K-W-L chart. Next, generate and record questions learners have about the topic. Finally, ask learners to read the text and note what they have learned.

Students can also use this strategy on their own by following this three-step process:

1. Identify—What do I already know?

2. Determine—What questions do I want answered?

3. As you read—Think about what I am learning.

Herrmann, Garfinkel, & Batdorf

Text Structure

Text structure refers to the pattern an author uses to create text. Narrative and expository are two common types of text with two distinctly different patterns of writing. Narrative text is writing in which a person tells a story—actual or fictional—in prose or verse. It is usually created for entertainment purposes. Examples of narrative text include stories, plays, and poems. A typical pattern of writing used to create narrative text includes these steps: (1) establishing a setting, (2) introducing characters, (3) describing a problem or conflict, (4) describing events related to resolving the problem or conflict, and (5) resolving the problem or conflict. You may want to experiment with some of the activities on the following pages to help your learners better understand narrative text.

Story Pyramid

You can help learners build a "sense of story" about narrative text by creating a "Story Pyramid" (adapted from a story mapping technique by Beck, 1979) to guide them as they organize information about characters, setting, and plot. Ask your learners to read a story and complete the following:

Line 1: one-word name of a character in the story
Line 2: two words that describe the setting
Line 3: three words that describe a character
Line 4: four words in a sentence that describe an event
Line 5: five words in a sentence that describe another event

The resulting story pyramid for "The Three Pigs" would look something like this:

Wolf
Straw house
Huffing, puffing, determined
He blew it down
Pig puts wolf in pot

Building Characteristics

Story Frame

Learners with more advanced reading and writing abilities can expand on the Story Pyramid activity by using a "Story Frame" (Fowler, 1982) to develop their comprehension skills. You'll need a complete narrative text and a story frame (shown below)

Important idea or plot

In this story the problem starts when_____

_____.

After that, _____

_____.

Next, _____

_____.

Then, _____

_____.

The problem is finally solved when _____

_____.

The story ends _____

_____.

Reprinted by permission from Fowler (1982).

Procedure:

1. Present the story frame to students before reading the story.
2. Read the frame with learners, noting the blank spaces they are supposed to complete.
3. Ask learners to read the story.
4. Ask learners to complete the story frame independently, using information from the story.
5. After learners complete the story frame; help them evaluate how well they've captured the sense of the story by reviewing the narrative text.

Story Parts

The Story Parts activity (adapted from Routman, 1991) helps learners recognize and be able to point out elements of a story. After reading a story, article, or book, ask learners to write down story element categories as shown below. Explain that well-written stories contain these elements. Ask learners to supply information for each category by referring to the story. (Interpretations may vary.)

Book or Story Title

Setting:

Characters:

Problem:

Events:

   1.

   2.

   3.

   4.

Resolution:

Venn Diagram

As suggested by Routman (1991), learners can use a Venn Diagram to compare two books, two versions of a story, or a story told in two different mediums, such as a book and a videotape, as shown in the example below.

First, draw two interconnecting circles. Above each circle label the medium that will have ideas listed in that circle. Next, list all ideas and events learners mention about each of the items being compared. Common ideas and events are placed in the overlapping area of the two circles:

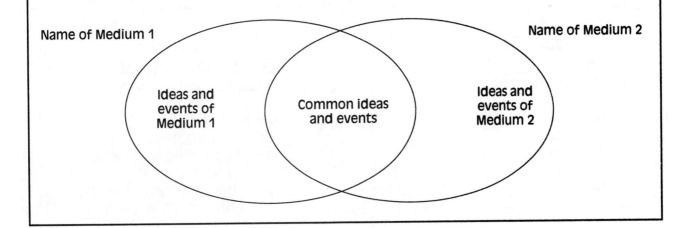

Personality Poem

Pam Hudson of Crowder College in Neosho, Missouri, developed an activity called "Personality Poem." Its purpose is to develop readers' understanding of characterization and descriptive writing. After reading a book or story, ask learners to describe different characters. Ask learners to write a personality poem about a favorite character using the following format:

    line 1: name
    line 2: two words describing his or her personality
    line 3: four words describing his or her looks
    line 4: five things he or she likes
    line 5: one word describing him or her

A sample poem is provided below.

> Ma Tuck from *Tuck Everlasting*
> Ma
> kind, compassionate
> great potato, floppy hat
> reunions, cooking, eating, fussing, fishing
> soft

Story Impression Strategy

The Story Impression Strategy (adapted from McGinley & Denner, 1987) can help learners predict story structure by forming an impression of how characters and events are interrelated.

First, choose key words and phrases from a story to serve as clues to making predictions. Then list words and phrases sequentially under "Story Impressions." Ask learners to predict what the story will be about through the use of the clue words. List these as "predictions." Ask learners to read the passage and compare predictions to the actual text. The resulting lists would look something like this:

Little Red Riding Hood

Story Impressions	Predictions
Forest	One day in the forest
Little Red Riding Hood	Little Red Riding Hood
Wolf	met a mean wolf
visited	who visited
grandmother	her grandmother
dressed up	he got dressed up like her grandmother
woodcutter	and then a woodcutter came and I predict they lived happily ever after.

Story Mapping Through Circular Pictures

Try Story Mapping (Routman, 1991) to help learners put events of a story into sequence.

1. After reading a story or book, ask the learners to draw a brief sketch of the beginning of the story in the 1 o'clock position of a large circle with twelve blank boxes (see example below).
2. Ask learners to continue drawing the main events of the story in a clockwise fashion, ending with the final picture in the 12 o'clock position.
3. Ask the learners to explain their decisions about main events.

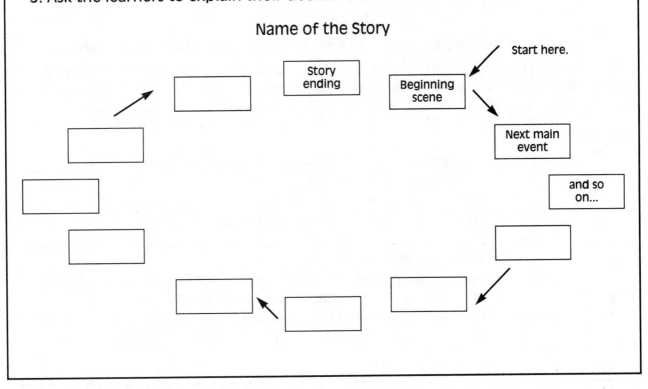

Name of the Story

Echo Reading

"Echo Reading" (Heckelman, 1969) is another way students can build confidence and fluency. It will also give them practice in reading with proper expression. Start simply by reading a line of text. Then ask learners to repeat the same line. With young children or nonreaders, point to each line of text as it is read and encourage learners to do the same. As learners begin to use expression and read more fluently, encourage independent reading.

Expository text is another common text structure. It is usually created to inform or persuade. Examples of expository text include textbook chapters, newspaper articles, and reference material. A typical pattern of expository text is introduction, body, and conclusion.

You can help your readers become more familiar with expository text by using the SQ3R strategy (Robinson, 1961). This strategy will also help your learners understand and recall information they read.

SQ3R: Survey, Question, Read, Recite, Review

The SQ3R strategy (Robinson, 1961) can be used with expository text to help learners understand and recall what they read. Provide ample opportunities for learners to use this strategy with a variety of reading materials. Diminish support as learners become more independent with using it. Discuss each of the following steps with learners:

Survey — the learner previews the material to develop a general outline for organizing information.

Question — the learner raises questions with the expectation of finding answers in the material to be studied.

Read — the learner next attempts to answer the questions formulated in the previous step.

Recite — the learner deliberately attempts to answer out loud or in writing the questions formulated in the second step.

Review — the learner reviews the material by rereading portions of the assignment in order to verify the answers given during the previous step.

Successful readers and writers understand the different patterns of narrative and expository text. If your learners can recognize text structures, they will understand more when they read and be able to create text that is easier to understand. (Both narrative and expository texts are explained in more detail in Chapter 4.)

Purposes for Reading and Writing

The ability to set purposes for reading and writing is an important element in learning to comprehend and create text. Successful readers and writers know how to establish a clear reason for reading or writing. For example, before going to vote in an upcoming election, a person may spend more time than usual reading newspaper articles that outline different candidates' positions on a controversial issue. In this case, the reader's purpose for reading is to gather important information before deciding which candidate to choose. On the other hand, if the same person were stuck in a garage waiting for a car to be fixed, the same newspaper article might be read simply for entertainment to pass the time more quickly. Regardless of the situation, setting purposes for reading or writing helps keep the reader or writer focused on the topic and task at hand.

Ability to Understand How Reading and Writing Work

Effective readers and writers understand written symbols—letters and words—associated with language. They also know the rules governing their use—such as how letters form words. We use routine skills and thinking and reasoning abilities to interpret text and to create meaning when we read and write.

Routine Skills

Routine skills are automatically applied with little thought or reasoning during reading or writing. Three types of routine skills are necessary for successful reading and writing. First, successful readers and writers understand letter-sound relationships. This means that when they read or write they automatically associate specific sounds with specific letters and letter combinations. Common letter-sound relationships are shown in Figure 1.

To better understand how the knowledge of letter-sound relationships is used during reading, consider the passage below taken from a popular travel magazine:

Figure 1
Common Letter-Sound Relationships

Consonants—*b, c, d, f, g, h, j, k, l, m, n, p, q, r, s, t, v, w, x, y, z.* All but the letters *c* and *g* have corresponding sounds that are quite consistent in English. The letters *c* and *g* have two sounds: hard (as in *cane, cat, go,* or *good*) and soft (as in *cent, city, gene,* or *gem*).

Consonant blends—A consonant blend or cluster combines two or three consecutive consonants. When the blend is pronounced, each letter has its own distinct sound. The following blends occur frequently in English: *bl, br, cl, cr, dr, fl, fr, gl, gr, pl, pr, sc, sk, sm, sn, sp, st, str, sw, tr,* and *tw.*

Consonant digraphs—Two consecutive consonants that represent a single sound are called consonant digraphs, as in the following examples: *ch, ck, ng, ph, sh, th,* and *wh.* The *th* may be voiced (*there, this*) or voiceless (*thin, thing*)—if your vocal cords vibrate, it is voiced; if they do not, it is voiceless.

Silent consonants—Certain consonants sometimes have no sound in spoken English, as in *gh* in *ghost, gn* in *gnat, kn* in *knot, ps* in *psalm,* or *rh* in *rhubarb.*

Vowels—There are two categories of vowel sounds that occur most frequently in English: long vowels such as *ate, eel, ice, rode,* or *use*; and short vowels such as *am, end, ill, odd,* or *us.*

Vowel digraphs—Two consecutive vowels with one sound are called vowel digraphs. The following are examples of the most common vowel digraphs: r*ai*n, *Au*gust, *ea*sy, m*ee*t, p*ie*, b*oa*t, t*oe*, and tr*ue.*

Diphthongs—Two consecutive vowels with a sound in which the tongue starts in one position and moves rapidly to another—such as *oi*l, b*oy*, or *out*—are called diphthongs.

Schwa—The schwa sound can best be described as an unstressed short *u*. It is symbolized phonetically by /ə/. The schwa sound is the most frequently occurring vowel sound in English and occurs with all vowels, as in com*a*, beat*e*n, im*i*tate, butt*o*n, and col*u*mn.

Adapted from Duffy, G.G., & Sherman, G.B. (1972). *Systematic reading instruction.* New York: HarperCollins.

Consonant:
A letter representing sounds made when one or more articulators constricts, stops, or diverts or obstructs the air flow.

Blend:
Joining sounds represented by two or more letters with minimal change in those sounds.

Digraph:
Two letters that represent one speech sound.

Herrmann, Garfinkel, & Batdorf

Four blasts on the whistle, and it's time to move out on the last leg, to Chama. We choose again to take the outdoor car, which, this time, is right behind the tender. It's an open freight car in which we stand, elbows on the railing, while the engine belches vast burps of black smoke and soot straight into our faces. Water from the tender sprinkles us occasionally like ocean spray under a sky as blue as eternity (Page, 1992, p. 52).

When a successful reader comes to the word *Chama* he or she automatically pronounces the *ch* at the beginning the same way as it sounds in the word *chair.* That is the sound commonly associated with the letters *ch* when they are combined at the beginning of a word. Your students can learn to pronounce letter combinations with little thought by practicing the activities for improving letter-sound relationships that follow.

Newspaper Activity

The "Newspaper Activity," as described by Janet Lambert of Eastern Illinois University in Charleston, helps students reinforce consonants, digraphs, and blends.

The procedure follows:

1. Gather newspaper advertisements that contain both a picture and the correct name of the object. Ask learners to locate objects and their accompanying words that begin with a designated letter sound.
2. On a large piece of construction paper, create and label several columns with headings such as food, clothing, and furniture.
3. Ask learners to cut out and mount each picture with its name in the appropriate column on the construction paper. Write the object's name if it is not printed in the newspaper.
4. Ask learners to point to and read their contributions to the poster. Emphasize the visual and auditory similarities of the beginning sounds of each word as the learners repeat the words.
5. Ask learners to copy these words into a personal dictionary (a looseleaf notebook) and read them aloud using the pictures and clues on the poster.

Parts of speech: Classes into which words have traditionally been categorized—noun, pronoun, verb, adjective, adverb, preposition, conjunction, and interjection.

The second set of routine skills successful readers and writers employ involves the basic rules governing the language. For example, those learning to read in English must know that reading or writing in English follows a left-to-right and top-to-bottom pattern. They must also be familiar with grammar and usage rules, parts of speech, and punctuation. Knowledge of these basic rules helps individuals understand written text and create cohesive text in which all of these elements work together in a meaningful way.

Third, successful readers and writers instantly recognize many short words used frequently in written language. A list of these "sight words" is shown in Figure 2.

For example, consider again the passage about Chama. Note how many times little words such as *on, to, is, and, in, a, of,* and *the* appear in the passage.

> Four blasts <u>on</u> <u>the</u> whistle, <u>and</u> it's time <u>to</u> move out <u>on</u> <u>the</u> last leg, <u>to</u> Chama. We choose again <u>to</u> take <u>the</u> outdoor car, which, this time, <u>is</u> right behind <u>the</u> tender. It's <u>an</u> open freight car <u>in</u> which we stand, elbows <u>on</u> <u>the</u> railing, while <u>the</u> engine belches vast burps <u>of</u> black smoke <u>and</u> soot straight into our faces. Water from <u>the</u> tender sprinkles us occasionally like ocean spray under <u>a</u> sky <u>as</u> blue <u>as</u> eternity.

These little words make up more than 25 percent of the entire passage! If these words are automatically recognized on sight, a certain amount of fluency is achieved; if they are not, reading can be slowed to an unproductive rate. Some activities for improving fluency follow.

Choral Reading

"Choral Reading" (Tierney, Readence, & Dishner, 1990) is a strategy used to foster the acquisition of vocabulary and fluency. It can also help your learners build confidence.

Ask learners to sit slightly in front of you and together hold the reading material. Have learners read along with you. Your voice should be slightly louder and faster than the learners' in the beginning. As the learners begin to master the material and gain confidence in saying the words, soften your voice or lag slightly behind. If the learners falter, reinforce them by increasing loudness and speed.

Herrmann, Garfinkel, & Batdorf

Figure 2
Basic Sight Words

Easiest	More Difficult	Still More Difficult	Most Difficult
I	house	feet	else
and	dog	many	nothing
the	ball	your	already
a	pretty	color	hello
to	water	family	more
one	old	milk	both
on	by	friend	animal
is	how	ask	large
you	day	read	learn
but	with	should	across
or	off	because	through
			answer

Adapted from Duffy, G.G., & Sherman, G.B. (1972). *Systematic reading instruction*. New York: HarperCollins.

Repeated Readings

The method of "Repeated Readings" (Samuels, 1979) can help learners see progress in their rate and fluency. It will also help them improve their sight vocabulary and confidence.

Follow this procedure:

1. Select an easy passage of 50 to 200 words.

2. Ask learners to read the selection. Discretely keep track of the time and errors. Record these later on a graph.

3. Ask learners to read the same passage during three sessions. Compare their errors on a graph, as shown below.

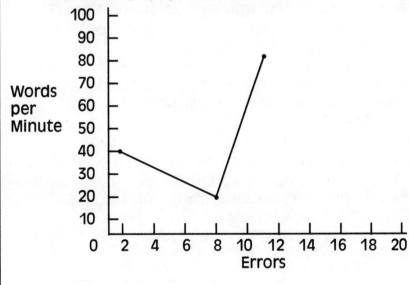

Read Alouds

Jeanne Shay Schumm, coauthor of the next chapter, uses "Read Alouds" to provide learners with opportunities to have book-sharing experiences. This activity can also be used to increase learners' exposure to and appreciation of literature and improve fluency in reading.

First try reading to learners by following the suggestions below. Then exchange roles and have learners read to you.

Tutor Reads to Learners

1. Before the session, choose a book slightly above the learners' reading level that you think they will enjoy. Select books with strong characters that you can present using different voices and actions. Practice reading the book before sharing it with learners.

2. Prepare learners for the reading by setting some guidelines for listening. Think ahead about the type of behavior that will make the reading session successful and discuss it with the learners. Before reading, allow learners to look at the cover and title page. Talk together about the author and illustrator. Ask questions about the book topic to activate learners' prior knowledge. Ask learners to predict what the story might be about.

3. Read slowly so learners can follow what you are reading. Remember, make the characters, mood, and action come alive for the learners. Encourage learners to ask questions and share thoughts about the events in the story. If you are not able to finish the story in one session, be sure to stop at a turning point in the plot so learners will look forward to the next session.

4. After you have finished reading, allow learners a minute to savor the experience. Pose questions in a discussion format and encourage learners to share their reactions to the story. Share your own reactions. Point out interesting details and ask learners to tell about the most enjoyable parts. Ask learners to retell the story. Extend the story by creating a sequel with the learners or by asking them to compose an alternate ending.

Learners Read to Tutor

1. Choose easy reading material. Too many new words will frustrate learners.

2. Allow learners to suggest familiar books or stories. As trust develops, encourage learners to attempt more challenging material.

3. Encourage younger children or nonreaders to "read" the story in their own words or to read the pictures. Do not try to correct mispronunciations or differences between the learners' language and the actual printed words. Provide help when learners ask for it.

4. It may be necessary to show reluctant readers how to read each page correctly. Then ask them to read the same page.

5. Encourage learners to do repeated readings. For the first reading, ask learners to concentrate on new words or difficult concepts. Ask learners to reread to improve fluency.

6. Motivate learners to reread a second or third time. Audiotape readings so learners can hear progress.

Finally, successful readers and writers know the meanings of many words. This knowledge is actively used to understand and create text about many different topics. To illustrate this point, make a list of all of the words you know the meaning of that are associated with the concept of "school." Chances are you will fill a piece of paper with words in a matter of minutes. Knowledge of word meanings plays an important role in constructing meaning during reading and creating cohesive text. A good strategy for improving vocabulary and knowledge of relationships among words and ideas follows.

Semantic Webbing

Semantic webbing (Freedman & Reynolds, 1980) or mapping can be used as a prewriting activity to help students organize ideas. The procedure follows:

1. Together with learners, choose a topic to be webbed.
2. Place the topic in the center of a piece of paper and circle it.
3. As ideas are generated, list them in circles that stem from the circled topic, as shown below.
4. After reading about the topic, add additional ideas to the web.
5. Use the web to create a first draft.

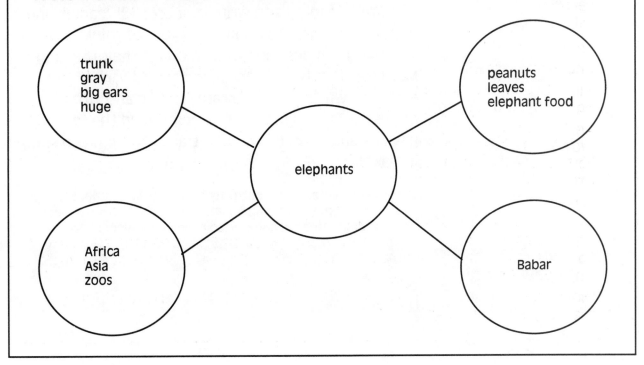

Thinking and Reasoning

In addition to using routine skills, successful readers and writers know how to think and reason before, during, and after reading and writing. For example, before reading or writing, they know how to activate their prior knowledge and use it to make sense out of what they are reading or to create text that makes sense. To illustrate this point, complete the following writing task:

> Write one sentence about the last time you drove a car. Keep track of your thinking as you write the sentence. Now write one sentence about how to make a good landing in a small airplane.

The sentence about driving a car was probably much easier for you to write than the second sentence because you probably have much more prior knowledge about driving cars than you do about flying airplanes. Consciously thinking about your prior knowledge as you attempted to write the sentence is what helped you decide what to write, how to phrase it, and how much to include in the sentence. Try writing another sentence about driving a car without first thinking about your prior knowledge and you will find it virtually impossible.

During reading and writing, successful readers and writers know how to apply two types of thinking and reasoning abilities. First, they monitor their thinking. More specifically, they are consciously aware of the extent to which what they are reading and writing makes sense. To illustrate this point, read the following passage and consciously keep track of how much sense it makes.

> The two kittens were perfectly content to stay under the bed until the quiet thunderstorm started. When it was over, the dogs came out and started eating their dinner again.

How long did it take you to realize the passage wasn't making sense? Thunderstorms generally are not quiet, so it was probably at that point that you first started to say, "Huh? This doesn't make sense!" That is how successful readers monitor their thinking during reading and writing.

In addition, successful readers and writers know how to reason strategically during reading or writing, especially when confusion occurs. For example, read the following passage and keep track of what you do if you become confused.

> The rotation in a Piper Cherokee occurs at 60 miles an hour. When achieving that IAS, apply back pressure on the yoke and step on the right rudder. Soon you will achieve you best angle of climb. (Duffy & Roehler, 1989, p. 39)

Probably you became confused when reading this passage because of its many unfamiliar uses of familiar words, such as "rotation" and "yoke." In this case, you may have tried to restore meaning by reasoning strategically with your prior knowledge about flying and clues provided by surrounding words. In another case when you encounter a word you cannot pronounce, you might try to figure it out by reasoning strategically about meaningful parts at the beginning or end of the word, while at the same time applying your knowledge of letter-sound associations contained in the word. Use the Mental Modeling technique described in Chapter 2 to teach this type of reasoning.

After reading and writing, successful readers and writers reflect on what they have read or written by *summarizing* or *drawing conclusions,* and *critically evaluating* what they have read or written by thinking about facts, bias, propaganda, or validity of conclusions. Thinking and reasoning in this way after reading and writing helps readers better understand what they have read and helps writers clarify what they have written.

A Final Word

This chapter has described three characteristics of effective readers and writers. Successful readers and writers (1) have a positive attitude toward self and reading and writing, (2) understand what they read and can create text that can be understood by others, and (3) know how to think and reason before, during, and after reading and writing. Becoming more familiar with the extent to which your learners possess these abilities and characteristics will help you develop effective instructional goals for tutoring.

References

Beck, I.L., McKeown, M.G., McCaslin, E., & Burket, A. (1979). *Instructional dimensions that may affect reading comprehension: Examples of two commercial reading programs.* Pittsburgh, PA: University of Pittsburgh Language Research and Development Center.

Duffy, G.G., & Roehler, L.R. (1989). *Improving classroom reading instruction: A decision-making approach.* New York: Random House.

Duffy, G.G., & Sherman, G.B. (1972). *Systematic reading instruction.* New York: HarperCollins.

Fowler, G.L. (1982). Developing comprehension skills in primary students through the use of story frames. *The Reading Teacher, 36*(2), 176-179.

Freedman, G., & Reynolds, E.G. (1980). Enriching basal reader lessons with semantic webbing. *The Reading Teacher, 33*(6), 677-684.

Heckelman, R.G. (1969). A neurological-impress method of remedial-reading instruction. *Academic Therapy, 4*, 277-282.

McGinley, W.J., & Denner, P.R. (1987). Story impressions: A prereading/writing activity. *Journal of Reading, 31*(3), 248-253.

Ogle, D.M. (1986). K-W-L: A teaching model that develops active reading of expository text. *The Reading Teacher, 39*(6), 564-570.

Page, J. (1992, July/August). Clattering through God's country. *National Geographic Traveler*, 50-53.

Robinson, F.P. (1961). *Effective study* (rev. ed.). New York: HarperCollins.

Routman, R. (1991). *Invitations: Changing as teachers and learners K-12.* Portsmouth, NH: Heinemann.

Samuels, S.J. (1979). The method of repeated readings. *The Reading Teacher, 32*(4), 403-408.

Stauffer, R.G. (1969). *Teaching reading as a thinking process.* New York: HarperCollins.

Tierney, R.J., Readence, J.E., & Dishner, E.K. (1990). *Reading strategies and practices.* Boston, MA: Allyn and Bacon.

CHAPTER 4

Helping Learners Complete Assigned Work

Jeanne Shay Schumm
Kathleen A. Hinchman

Scenario one: Nalini Singh agreed to work in Ms. Thompson's fifth grade class as a parent volunteer. Ms. Thompson is concerned about three students, Frederick, Melinda, and Charley, who are having difficulty passing social studies and science tests. Nalini's job is to provide the students with one-to-one tutoring in these content area subjects.

Scenario two: Earle Thomas is a third-year college student majoring in public administration. As part of the college's community action program, Earle has volunteered to tutor middle school students in an after-school program at a local YMCA. Earle will be responsible for helping youngsters complete regular homework assignments and study for tests.

Scenario three: Janet Parker, a computer programmer, has volunteered through her local school district to help adults learn the reading and writing skills necessary to earn their high school equivalency diploma. She spends two evenings a week at a local elementary school helping adult learners practice specific reading and writing tasks recommended by the school district.

In some tutoring programs, volunteers take on the primary responsibility for learners' literacy progress. In this case, a tutor might be expected to assess learners' status, to organize and provide instruction suited to learners' identified needs, and to gauge learners' progress. Thus, the tutor may be required to participate in a fairly extensive training program or to otherwise study techniques for teaching and assessing reading, writing, and other subject areas.

But what about the individual who volunteers to help students with assigned work? Settings where this occurs include elementary and secondary classrooms where tutors help learners complete school work. Tutors may also work with teachers in adult-education settings where learners are working to develop basic skills or pass a high school equivalency examination. Tutors might also volunteer at an after-school latchkey program where learners bring school work, questions, and a general idea of areas where they need extra help. Tutors may or may not have access to teachers' assistance in this type of program.

Nalini, Earle, and Janet in the scenarios above, like many other tutors, are involved because they want to help students succeed. Also like many other tutors, Nalini, Earle, and Janet are not quite certain where to begin. They want to provide support but not "do" the work for the students. They want to help their students learn but are not confident that what they might teach is "consistent" with what teachers are presenting in classes today. They want to help learners study, but they don't feel familiar with effective study techniques. The purpose of this chapter is to provide volunteers like Nalini, Earle, and Janet with specific strategies for assisting learners with work that has been assigned by someone else. We have included information about the context within which work is assigned and how to get started within this context. In addition, the chapter contains recommendations for helping learners complete routine assignments, pull important information from textbooks and class lectures, prepare for tests, and complete writing assignments and long-term projects. Emphasis is placed on how to fit into existing programs and on teaching learners how to learn independently.

Understanding the Context

When volunteers tutor in settings where a classroom teacher is present, the teacher holds primary responsibility for learners' instruction. A tutor in this type of setting usually helps learners complete instructional activities organized by the teacher. The rationale for complet-

Schumm & Hinchman

ing such activities may be clear, so that tutor, teacher, and learner understand what is to be accomplished. Sometimes program requirements are very straightforward, and skilled teachers have time to share explanations thoroughly with students and tutors. In other cases, activities may be less than clear for a variety of reasons. The rationale for an activity may be tied to an understanding on the part of the teacher that is not shared by a tutor. The teacher may not have the time or inclination to explain this understanding to a part-time volunteer. Perhaps the teacher's reasoning is anchored in beliefs about learning unknown to the tutor or learner or in conflict with those of the tutor or learner. Sometimes a learner and tutor interact in ways that differ from what the teacher might have predicted, making an activity less clear.

No matter what the circumstance, it is important for volunteers to remember that a teacher who carries responsibility for learning has the final authority to make decisions about what will happen to facilitate that learning. Volunteers should recognize the expertise teachers develop from studying and working in settings over time. Teachers know about individual students, about the interactions among individuals, and about the larger context of the settings in which they work. Managing a class full of learners on a day-to-day basis is no easy task, and volunteers should make their entries into teachers' worlds with full respect for this responsibility.

Due to the one-to-one nature of a tutor's work, the volunteer may have the opportunity to perceive a learner in a more intimate way than is possible for the regular teacher. There is a greater chance the tutor will notice quickly when a learner is experiencing a particular difficulty, an approach does not seem to be working, or another way of explaining might work better. The tutor may also be in a position to implement an alternative approach in response to specific observations. A tutor may, in fact, be able to determine a better way to the same end.

Good teachers whose goal is students' progress will always welcome suggestions and sincere efforts—especially if they are offered in a manner sensitive to what the teacher has been trying to accomplish and to the years of study and experience that feed these attempts. What will be a problem, however, are tutors who suggest that what teachers are doing is wrong or the result of bad judgment. A teacher in this situation may think, justifiably, that it is not productive for learners to see primary service providers as incompetent or discredited in any way. Tutors need to be "politicians" in the most sincere sense, inviting themselves into the world of learners and teachers in a manner that shows respect for what has come before the tutor arrived and what will come after he or she is gone.

Getting Started

A brand new experience with a new tutor offers learners the opportunity for a fresh start. A new tutor represents hope for a more positive experience with learning tasks that require reading and writing. The suggestions provided in Chapter 1 of this book will help you adjust to your role and establish a positive working relationship with learners. However, we would like to offer additional suggestions as you begin to help your learners with assigned work.

Before the First Tutoring Session

Before you begin tutoring, arrange a conference with the person responsible for supervising the tutorial program. This may be a program director, school administrator, or classroom teacher. The purposes of this conference are to clarify your duties, determine what is expected of you, and let you know how what you do fits in to the total program. If the person in charge does not suggest such a meeting, ask for one anyway. The following issues should be discussed.

- Relationship with the classroom teacher
    Find out if you will be able to talk with the learners' teacher. Students with learning problems are not always clear about assignments and tests. A conference with the teacher may help you

Schumm & Hinchman

become oriented to specific expectations and routines for handling assignments and tests. The teacher can help you focus on particular areas where learners need help and areas that will provide the most immediate classroom success. He or she can also help you set realistic goals.

- Relationship with parents

    Parents often want to be informed of their children's progress during tutoring sessions. Also, you may be able to provide parents with suggestions for supporting and extending tutoring sessions in the home. However, it is important to inform program administrators about your parent communications. Otherwise, a five-way miscommunication among tutor, learner, parent, teacher, and program director may occur. At the outset of your tutoring experience, make certain that communication lines are clear.

- Learning about your learners

    Before you meet with your learners for the first time, find out all you can about them. Talk to the program director or classroom teacher. Questions about academic and behavioral characteristics are appropriate as well as questions about the learners' family backgrounds, interests, and hobbies. Some adults you interview may be negative, but you should try to remain open-minded. Remember, your learners are looking to you for a fresh start.

- Trouble-shooting

    Know where to go if you have problems with learners' behavior or if learners do not seem to be making the progress you expect. You should not be expected to handle situations like these alone.

- Record-keeping

    Ask what records of tutoring sessions must be kept. If nothing is required, a simple tutoring log may help you keep track of what was covered during sessions.

- What to do if there is nothing to do

     Sometimes learners forget to bring books or assignments to tutoring sessions. Establish a clear plan for how best to use the tutoring time in such cases. If a tutoring session is canceled because there is nothing to do, your learners may have invented an effective means for avoiding the sessions.

The First Tutoring Session

Your primary goal during the first tutoring session is to set the tone for a positive relationship that will enhance learning. Spend some time getting to know your learners. Start by finding out about their personal interests and hobbies. Share some information about yourself as well. A good ice-breaker activity is the "biopoem," described in what follows.

Biopoem

You can use this activity (submitted by Pam Hudson of Crowder College in Neosho, Missouri) to get to know learners by observing the content of their writing. Ask the learners to write a poem about themselves using the following format:

line 1, first name
line 2, four adjectives describing yourself
line 3, "Lover of (three things)"
line 4, "Who gives (three things)"
line 5, "Who fears (three things)"
line 6, "Who would like to see (three things)"
line 7, "Resident of _____ "
line 8, last name

Encourage learners to modify their poems, if they'd like. The following sample poem uses the basic format but adds a few lines.

Pam
Happy, excitable, plain, nosey
Mother of Callie, Casey, Tal, and Georgia
Lover of chocolate, books, students
Who feels overwhelmed, fortunate, fabulous
Who needs Diet Cherry Coke, Bob, friends
Who gives lectures, love, attention
Who fears snakes, Dr. Farnsworth, the checkbook
Who would like to see Hawaii, the pyramids, God
Resident of Neosho
Hudson

Ask questions to find out what your learners think about school, different school subjects, and concerns about completing assignments and taking tests. At the beginning it's important to listen—especially to your learners' likes and dislikes pertaining to school. Try not to provide lots of advice initially—just listen.

Explain to your learners what they can expect of you during tutoring sessions. For example, your learners should know that you will arrive on time, give them your undivided attention during the tutoring session, do your best to help them become even more successful learners, allow some time during the tutoring session for personal talk (but insist on time being focused on assigned work), start each session by establishing goals and agenda with the learners, and end each session by evaluating with the learners what went right, what went wrong, and what needs to be done differently next time.

You can help develop a sense of trust with your learners by letting them know what you are expected to report to teachers and parents. It is not likely that a sense of trust will develop if your learners think you will talk behind their backs. Inform your learners that if you have something to report, you will do your best to tell them first.

Finally, find out how your learners currently keep track of assignments. If they do not have a system, then as your first collaborative effort, brainstorm ways to accomplish this task. There are numerous ways to keep track of assignments, such as calendars, notepads, and assignments sheets. Let your learners decide which way would work best.

Helping Learners with Routine Assignments

Much of the work you do with your learners may be assisting with routine assignments or homework. This can include answering textbook questions and exercises, solving mathematics problems, defining words, or completing worksheets. Your learners' goals will probably be simply to get the homework done. Your goal should be to help them understand how to complete the task so that in the future they can work independently. The following general guidelines can help you move your student toward independence:

1. Concentrate on how to read directions. Show your learners how to break multistep directions into components. Many times learners do not do well on homework simply because they do not understand the directions.

2. Think about process as well as product. The product is the finished homework. The process is how the answers or solutions were derived. For as many items as seems reasonable, if your learners got the answer right, ask them how they did it. This will help reinforce the process they used. If your learners got the answer wrong, ask them to explain their reasoning. Then offer an alternate way by saying, "I understand what you were thinking. Let's try looking at it another way."

3. Find out the teacher's policy on correcting homework. Some teachers think of homework as an opportunity for independent practice and then look at learners' mistakes to see if further instruction is necessary. Be clear about the teacher's use of homework and whether or not you should correct your learners' work.

4. Avoid doing the work for your learners. Sometimes this might be a real temptation. It is certainly advisable to demonstrate how to solve problems or work together with your learners to understand key concepts. However, try to help your learners strive toward independence. When they have to take a test in class, you will not be there to help.

Helping Learners Prepare for Tests

Test preparation actually includes three steps. The first is deciding what is important to learn and predicting what will be on the test. Typically learners use textbooks, class notes, and reflection about lectures and discussions to decide what to study. The second step is developing study tools, such as flashcards or outlines, that can help organize the information to be learned. The third step is practice, focusing on rehearsal and memorization of key ideas. Your learners may need help gaining independence in one or more of these steps. In this section we provide some hints for accomplishing this goal.

Deciding What Is Important to Study

Pierre Salinger, U.S. President John Kennedy's press secretary, was once asked how he helped the president prepare for press conferences. He reported that his team predicted which questions would be asked and then provided support by reflecting about answers. Salinger remembered that the team was able to predict most questions, and for the questions they did not predict, the president had developed sufficient background information to cope with members of the press.

Most learners predict what will be on a test. It is not unusual after a test to overhear remarks such as "I didn't think she would ask that" or "I didn't even look at that section; I didn't know he thought that stuff was important" or "I sure guessed that one right—I'm glad I went over that section last night." Predicting questions may be systematic and intentional. For example, some learners may make up sample tests or ask a parent or friend to quiz them on key information. For most learners, however, prediction is incidental, incomplete, and incorrect. In many cases learners simply do not spend enough concentrated time focusing on the material to be learned, do not predict enough questions, and do not learn the answers to the questions. But learners also may have a tough time figuring out what the teacher thinks is important. The teacher has more prior knowledge about the topic, more interest in the topic, and a better understanding of district and state curriculum objectives. As a tutor, part of your role is to help learners prepare for tests—the classroom equivalent of Kennedy's press conference.

To get started you need some idea of what the teacher expects. The teacher probably will use information from the textbook, information presented in class lectures or discussions, or a combination of the two. First try to work with your learners to find out about their courses. If your learners do not know what is expected of them, make arrangements to ask the teacher. Second, ask your learners to bring you old tests. They may be reluctant to do so, particularly if grades were not satisfactory. Once again, talk to the teacher and ask to see old tests so you can get an idea of test format and level of detail. But remember: your goal should be to try to develop learners' independence. At the beginning you'll probably need to demonstrate effective reading and study strategies. Gradually let your learners work independently, but be there to provide support and encouragement.

Getting Information from the Textbook

Some teachers base chapter and unit tests on textbook information. Many textbook publishers supply teachers with tests, and teachers use these commercial tests rather than writing their own. When the teacher relies heavily on the textbook, it is important to help your learners figure out how to extract important information from the assigned reading material.

Typically the unit of study for tests in elementary, middle school, and high school is the textbook chapter. The best place to start is with a chapter preview. The purpose of a chapter preview is to get a general idea of the scope of the chapter and to decide how much of the chapter you can cover during your study period. To preview a chapter with your students, walk them through the reading material and examine the title, purpose of the chapter or chapter objectives, headings and subheadings, graphics and illustrations, words in boldface type or italics, summary, and questions at the end of the chapter. As you talk about each chapter element, determine informally what your learners know and what they don't know, what the teacher covered in class, and what causes the most problems for your learners. After you finish previewing (five minutes should be sufficient), agree on how much and which parts of the chapter you plan to cover during the study session. You might be able to cover the entire chapter, or it might be better to "chunk" the chapter into study sections.

Now you're ready to dig in! Work together to read the chapter section by section (silently or out loud—whatever you and your learners decide is best) and predict what might be on the test. You have the advantage of good reading skills and perhaps some prior knowledge of the topic; your learners have the advantage of having heard something about the topic in class. Take turns predicting questions and supplying the answers. You can use text features such as headings and boldface type identified during the preview to guide your predictions. Make certain your questions are about general key concepts, important vocabulary, and significant details. Predict as many questions as possible. When you get to the end of a section, summarize the most important ideas as a review. Ask your learners to identify areas they still find difficult to understand. You may also ask one another questions pertaining to your reactions to the material presented. Then move on to the next section.

If your learners have severe word-recognition problems or are English as a Second Language (ESL) learners, additional tutoring measures may be appropriate, such as reading the chapter aloud and answering questions as you read; audiotaping the chapter so learners can listen to the information over and over again; or simplifying the chapter content in the form of an outline or study flashcards.

English as a second language (ESL) learners:
Learners enrolled in English-speaking schools who need English-language instruction because they come from non–English-speaking backgrounds.

Getting Information from Class Notes

Because textbooks are simply too difficult for many learners, some teachers rely on lectures and class discussions as their primary instructional tools. In such cases, notetaking is critical. The question-prediction strategy mentioned above should apply to getting information from class notes. If your learners take neat, accurate, complete notes, then question-prediction should be straightforward. However, if your learners' notes are less than stellar or nonexistent, then your task is somewhat different—you need to provide instruction in notetaking.

Students just learning how to take notes often have a hard time deciding what to write. They either write too much or too little. They may have never seen a model of what class notes should look like, so they really do not know where to start. You can help by demonstrating effective notetaking and by providing structured opportunities for practice. One way to demonstrate notetaking is by using an audio- or videotaped lecture. As the audio- or videotape is playing, sit beside your learners and demonstrate how to take notes. The tape doesn't need to be long—five minutes should be sufficient. Have other tapes available so that your learners have opportunities for guided practice. After your learners have started making progress in notetaking, work with them to develop a system for taking notes in class and ask them to bring the notes to tutoring sessions.

It may be advisable to inform your learners' parents and teachers of the system so all parties are aware. You and your learners could write letters to parents and the teacher letting them know that you have been working on notetaking and the nature of your action plan. If necessary, find a way to get your learners new notebooks so they will have a fresh start.

Some learners still have problems with notetaking—even after lots of coaching. If your learners are having difficulty, arrange to have class lectures audiotaped and then listen to the tapes together. If the teacher does not agree to this arrangement, then ask if he or she will arrange for "study buddies" to be assigned to your learners. Study buddies can take class notes, and you and the teacher can arrange to have them photocopied for your study sessions.

Helping Learners Study

Many learners are rewarded for poor study habits. They easily remember what they read and hear, and they spend no time reviewing. They are then rewarded with tests consisting of recognition items that require little

Schumm & Hinchman

thought or understanding. There has been no need for them to move beyond automatic pilot to complete their test preparation.

Other learners fail tests because they have trouble remembering information, have limited prior knowledge to aid in the learning of new information, or were never in class in the first place. Gather together any group of youngsters—of almost any age, successful or not—and ask them how they get ready for a test and you will hear, "Read over the materials," "Read the chapters again," "Go over handouts from class," or "Study the teacher's review sheets."

Learners develop their approaches to studying from bits of advice provided by teachers and parents. They have heard such disparate offerings as "Turn off the music when studying," "Be sure to study the chapter and the review sheets," and "Don't wait until the last night." Seldom do you hear learners talk about strategy, about a systematic way of approaching the task of studying that does not require repetition of tasks already accomplished.

As a tutor, you may often find yourself in the position of helping your learners study for specific tests. You will also be concerned with helping your learners develop study skills they can use independently. Your goal is to help them develop a systematic, personalized approach to studying that will last through a lifetime of learning.

Repetition and quality of processing are two critical ingredients in remembering information. Rote repetition of an idea, definition, formula, or fact causes us to remember more easily. However, if we spend time thinking about what we are learning from many angles, making connections among pieces of information, working to gain a sense of the big picture, then new information is apt to become ours, and we will do well on any assessment of our understanding. You can make a number of recommendations to your learners that implement both these approaches to remembering. However, be honest—some courses will not require this level of effort, and their material is easily covered and remembered. Learners readily perceive this, and you will gain credibility for your realistic understanding of the classroom.

You will want to consider several other ideas as you help your learners prepare for tests. A discussion of some of these follows.

- Help learners get information the first time

  Learners should be encouraged to read and digest reading assignments as though they know they will be tested on them. Encourage them to listen to and record class lectures and discussions and to spend time reviewing information as it is collected.

- Help learners develop a system for organizing materials

  Materials for a course can accumulate in many places over the period of time between tests. Textbooks may be read and highlighted thoroughly and stuffed with dozens of important, but disorganized, papers. Review sheets may be at home in a pile on a desk. Study guides may be sitting at the bottom of a locker piled high with books, coats, and hair gel.

  Most of us have learned the hard way that it is easier to gather materials when they are contained in a common and safe place—a binder or folder of class and text notes, study guides, review sheets, and other class handouts—when they are first covered in class. Different techniques work for different learners. You may want to take a trip to a local school supply store and peruse the selections with your learners, talking about the advantages and disadvantages of each system. Be sure the learners check to see if the teacher has any particular requirements.

  Once a system is chosen, it must be implemented. It is most appropriate for a learner to spend a bit of time each day organizing materials as they are received. For example, several minutes each day can be spent—at home, at a tutoring session, in a study hall—punching holes in class handouts, organizing material in class binders, and reviewing materials as they are categorized.

Your learners will also want to spend a few minutes organizing once an actual test is announced. You can help your learners sift through a collection of material, ranking each item in terms of relative importance. Talk about the course and about daily class activities. Help learners find the materials that provide reference to the overall course and the teachers' expectations.

Some teachers distribute course outlines, and others circulate review sheets when a test is announced. Other teachers do not provide a handout, but it is apparent that their curriculum follows the ordering of the textbook. For still other teachers, learners will need to make their own list of topics covered. For these classes, the learners will need to discern what is most important from the amount of material presented and time spent on each topic.

You can talk with your learners in a way that classroom teachers cannot. It is important in the more intimate context of the tutoring partnership to talk about the fact that despite what learners think, most teachers are not out to trick them. Rather, most information is outlined and presented in a way that the teacher thinks is obvious. Teachers' views of curriculum order can be colored by many years of teaching the same course. In addition, some teachers are simply less well organized than others. In this case the learners' task is more difficult—they must guess what is in the teacher's head.

- Help learners match their study plan to the test type

Be sure your learners ask their teachers about the format for the test, time limits, materials needed, and topics covered. They can also ask the teacher how this test will compare with the previous test and how last year's students did.

- Look at your learners' previous tests

    Be sensitive in your approach, because no one likes to talk about weakness and failure. With the right relationship, however, you can talk together about the apparent strengths and weaknesses of the learners' approaches. You can derive possible explanations for particular performance. Did the test seem fair to the learners? Why? On what section of the test did the learners achieve the highest score? Lowest score? What are the possible explanations for this performance? Is there a particular type of question that the learners seem to have difficulty with, no matter what its content? Might a different kind of studying help learners do a better job on particular sections?

- Work together to develop a study schedule

    Once you and your learners agree that you have an understanding of what will be on a test, how it will be tested, and how the format fits in with their strengths and weaknesses, you can work together to develop a study schedule. As you would with any long-term project, consider the number of days available, the amount of time available each day, and other daily commitments. Look at the number of topics to be covered, consider the depth of understanding that seems to be required, and think about the learners' strengths. Divide topics into groups, leaving time on the last day or two to do a large-scale review of all the material—a chance to see how all the details fit into the "big picture".

    Remind your learners that studying a little bit each day can be more productive than reviewing material all at once. This way, learners can mull over content, questions, and how pieces of information fit together. If studying is paced well and begins early, the student will even have time to ask the teacher about newly discovered areas of difficulty or lack of understanding. When a course is especially difficult, these extra few minutes

Schumm & Hinchman

between original acquisition and review can make all the difference.

Talk with your learners about how to study differently for different types of tests. On true-false or multiple-choice tests, students must be able to seek and recognize the answer, eliminating both obvious and not-so-obvious distractors along the way. Such tests may require less study time. However, if the test requires short or long written responses, students may need to be able to remember complicated ideas and the facts that support them. They may also need to remember definitions or answers to questions about why or how things work the way they do. They will really need to "work" the material, gaining deep understanding of key concepts and supporting details.

- Help learners engage in constructive study

Rather than reading over material, learners will, with guidance, want to learn to engage in something a bit more active. In a topic-by-topic review, help them consolidate material, talking along the way about what the teacher seemed to consider the most important ideas and why.

Many students find that the most difficult part of studying for a test is compiling the text, lecture notes, study guides, and review sheets. Learners may want to do this by generating a central, summative study guide for review which will result in a deeper level of understanding and memory. Reconsider the information and how it fits together from several different angles. Talk together about meaning, and about what is likely to be on the test as you revise your summary sheets.

Another step that can be very helpful in constructive studying is using the summary to make up practice test questions. Few learners develop this strategy on their own, and this level of processing may be unnecessary for most of what learners will be tested on. But such review can cause anxious learners to feel relaxed and right at home once they are confronted with the test. Develop questions that mimic other questions the teacher has asked on tests. Consider, too, the announced format of the test. Use these questions to quiz students repeatedly and to organize review during the final days before the test.

- Provide secrets to successful test-taking

Anxious learners may feel more prepared if they know some of the tricks of test-taking before they sit down to the test. Give them practice tests if it is apparent that they have particular difficulty with some kinds of testing tasks. One such trick is something that learners sometimes ignore in their eagerness to get the task done—that is, learners should be sure to read the directions and ask questions about the task if anything is unclear. If one learner has a question, others probably have exactly the same question—or would if they read the directions and really thought about them. Some teachers have even resorted to giving away answers to obscure test items in the fourth or fifth sentence of the directions as a lesson to students who fail to read through them!

In most test formats, learners will want to look for information about where to write answers and in what form, how to think about wording of questions, and how extensively to state an answer. For example, on a multiple-choice test, learners will want to look for a distinction between "correct answer," "best answer," and "the one that is unlike the others."

Another secret to taking tests is pacing. Learners should find out exactly how much time is available to them. Then they should look through the test quickly, noting the format and some questions, and making guesses about the length of time that will be required for each section. Then they will need to pace themselves accordingly.

Some people like to do the hardest section first, thinking that their thoughts would be freshest and most critical early on. Others like to do the easiest questions first so they have more time for

Schumm & Hinchman

ones that might cause them difficulty. The choice is really the learner's. What is important is to consider time management and to continue to check on the clock as the test progresses.

Finally, it is important to talk together about your learners' guessing strategies. They should ask the teacher for advice. On some standardized tests, learners may be better off leaving blanks. On most teacher-made tests, however, learners have a fairly good chance of being rewarded with additional points if they guess well. On a true-false test, for example, there is at least a 50 percent chance of guessing correctly. In this case, be certain that your learners are not among the group that simply colors in a design when confronted with a test for which they are entirely unprepared.

Multiple-choice tests can be made easier with a strategy that narrows the odds by eliminating the obviously incorrect answers first. Learners can then consider the remaining choices.

The test-taker should also look for qualification in the language used in both multiple-choice and true-false items. Statements that seem to be overgeneralizations are apt to be incorrect or false: "Skies are *always* blue" or "Tests *are not* difficult." Longer answers containing more qualifiers are more likely to be true: "Skies are *usually* blue" or "Tests *can be* difficult." Another important point of logic concerning true-false and multiple-choice tests is that if an item seems partially false, then it is wholly false.

With essay tests, it is important for your students to remember that most of what can be accomplished will be of first-draft quality; this can be a frustration for learners who have been taught to write, revise, and edit their work over several drafts. Teachers don't expect answers on these tests to mirror polished essays, but your learners can still take time to organize their writing by brainstorming, clustering, or outlining as needed to gain some sense of the direction they'll take once they start writing.

Helping Learners Complete Writing Assignments

An assignment to compose a piece of writing may be given to your learners for a variety of reasons. A teacher may want them to share or clarify what they have learned by composing an explanation or story. Teachers also assign writing so learners can exercise creativity or simply practice writing.

Many of us do not have confidence in ourselves as writers. Many more of us simply do not like to write because we know the work it involves. Such personal feelings can affect us as tutors. It is important to remember that the invitation to help would not be extended if someone felt that you lacked the necessary skills. In addition, it can be very appropriate to talk with learners about your experiences and beliefs in realistic, truthful terms.

On the other hand, you may find that, for some reason, you disagree with a writing assignment a teacher has given. You may find that an assignment does not challenge your learners or offer them enough freedom to develop a piece of writing they really care about. In either case, it is important to remember that you must not undermine the teacher's goals.

You should understand that the process of writing can differ from one person to another. Approaches also depend on the kind of text being composed and the purpose of the assignment. As you help your learners with immediate writing assignments, consider how you can help them develop independence as writers.

Nurture Independent Writers

Anyone who has ever written anything—from a letter to a term paper to a published novel—knows that good writing does not flow onto paper whole and well formed. Instead, most writers proceed in fits and starts, searching for topics, tossing around ideas, drafting, revising, discarding, redrafting, and editing until an acceptable piece has been crafted. Even then, what is considered acceptable depends on the purpose and relative importance of the piece. You can help your learn-

Schumm & Hinchman

ers develop independence in writing by following a process for completing writing assignments.

Understanding how writing works.   Writing is a thinking process with several related components described as planning, drafting, revising, editing, and publishing. You should understand the thinking associated with these components so you don't try to tackle too much at once while you tutor. New writers should understand these steps in the writing process so they don't become frustrated by the work it takes to write a piece that communicates well. You can help learners develop this understanding by talking frequently about how writing works and by using the Mental Modeling technique described in Chapter 2.

The components of the writing process are not necessarily sequential. One writer may develop a plan and stick to it from the beginning. Another may begin most efficiently by simply putting pen to paper and starting to write; a plan for organizing the writing can be developed and refined once some ideas have been jotted down. A third writer may plan and draft a piece and set it aside—only to read it later and discover that it makes little sense. Be sure to recognize the individuality of the learners with whom you work and to help without smothering them if they struggle with any of the components.

Organizing thoughts on paper.   Brainstorming and clustering can help beginning authors who have difficulty organizing thoughts around a topic. Begin by talking with your learners about the value of different topics in terms of what the assignment requires. Discuss the purpose, audience, and form of the writing. You can serve as a naive interpreter of the learners' understandings about the scope and purpose of assignments. As a third party in the student-teacher assignment transaction, you can also talk together about task requirements, about the teacher's apparent expectations, and about what it takes to get a good grade on a piece of writing in this teacher's classroom.

Once your learners have selected a topic, work together to list everything that comes to mind about that topic. Look for categories into which the ideas on

Brainstorming:
The unrestrained offering of ideas or suggestions by all members of a group.

Clustering:
Creating groups and subgroups of highly correlated variables.

the list can be clustered. Organize the list into a diagram, illustrating possible relationships among the terms. Discuss how a piece of writing might be organized so clusters are reflected in the sentences, paragraphs, and sections.

Getting started.   One of the hardest tasks for any writer is simply getting started. You can help by having your learners tell you about topics that interest them. Encourage them to begin by writing what they are saying to you. Take dictation if necessary. Starting may even involve having the learners talk into a tape-recorder for later transcription as a first draft. Explain that anything can be revised. Informal talk can be made to look more formal, and sentences and paragraphs can be reorganized. The important element is to get ideas on paper.

Developing writing fluency.   Help learners develop writing fluency by having them keep a journal, diary, or daybook. Many learners simply have not had much practice with writing and consequently have not developed the ability to produce text fluently. Free writing—writing about whatever is in the author's head—can help to develop fluency. The context for such free writing might be a private journal. You can help by keeping a journal of your students' progress and sharing it with them. You might even keep a journal with individual learners in which you write to each other about events of the day, school work, or other things you both find interesting.

Understanding the revision process.   The first revision of a writing assignment can begin when a draft has been completed. The focus should be on getting the content down right. Is the content all there? Is it in the right order? Have points been made clearly, in a way that will be understandable to the intended audience? Is each paragraph on topic? What problems are you having? Do the beginning and ending do all that they could?

You may find that learners feel their first drafts are ready to hand in. To help them become more willing to revise, show them that writing is a process of communication. It is different from conversation because writers may be far away from their readers. Thus, writing is not typically at its best after one draft when it is most like talk written down. Professionals have editors and other writers to bounce ideas off of; it can take dozens of revisions before a piece is finally satisfactory for the intended audience. Teach your learners that part of revision might include storing or discarding a piece and starting over. This is an author's choice, although sometimes the pressure of completing school assignments on time can make this option seem less attractive.

A simple conference can be used to begin revisions. You can help by listening to your student read the newly composed text. Your distance from day-to-day class discussion allows you to listen objectively. To show respect for the effort it takes to construct text, you should listen carefully, making notes as needed but not interrupting the student. After the reading, first say what you liked about the writing and its content. Then repeat the points of the text as you understood them. Ask questions about parts of the text you didn't understand. It is the learner's job to decide whether or not the text communicates what was intended.

The emphasis of this type of interaction is on the message the learner is trying to communicate in the writing. Try to temper the sophistication of your observations, limit your questions, and avoid overly negative comments. Imagine yourself in the student's position; it is difficult to show a piece of writing to another person. Reserve talk about mechanics for another time, once the piece is closer to reaching its intent.

At some point your learner will have to tackle a writing assignment without you. You can help encourage independence by explaining how the learner can evaluate his or her own writing. If a writer plans ahead, a draft can be set aside for a few days and approached later with new objectivity and insight—much like a tutor who is able to make recommendations without preconceived notions. Students can add needed distance to the process by reading their own pieces aloud.

Organizing. You may wish to help your learners think about the organization of paragraphs and sections. To do this, it can be helpful to reoutline a piece as the author has drafted it, referring back to the original clustering as an additional point of reference. A tutor should also demonstrate the value of headings, sub-headings, and transition sentences—by sharing examples, writing a few with the learner, and discussing how the writer's own text may become more readable through the use of such devices.

It may be helpful for you to discuss interesting, effective beginnings. Share examples of topic sentences and discuss the idea that sometimes they can only be worded well once a piece is in its most complete form. In time, introduce learners to other writers' efforts to begin pieces in ways that grab and hold the reader's attention.

Polishing the product. A last step of the writing process is preparing material for publication—that is, for sending it off to its intended audience. To do this, help the learner decide if the strong content of the piece is mirrored in the way the conventions of writing are used. You will want to read over the piece together and look at mechanics, spelling, wording, and punctuation, checking especially for errors that will be noticed by other learners.

It may be tempting to simply "fix" less conventional spellings and wordings. However, this may mislead a teacher into thinking that a learner understands a set of rules that he or she really does not. You may also wish to take the opportunity to teach some element of mechanics with examples from the writing of others and with discussion of different approaches. This may be appropriate, as long as you do not overwhelm your learners. If they don't "get it," then it is probably the case that they are not ready to understand. They may not have seen the spelling or sentence construction frequently enough in print to understand and make it part of their developing repertoire.

It is important not to overemphasize mechanics. As many of us know, fear of error can greatly inhibit our

Schumm & Hinchman

ability to get our thoughts down in writing in the first place. As a tutor, you will not want to jeopardize your relationship—and your students' writing fluency—by spending too much time on correcting mechanical problems.

Understanding the difference between school writing and real writing. Teach your learners that writing for an audience of teachers can be complicated. In this case, the writer and reader may have already talked a great deal about the subject of the writing, and these conversations may lead the teacher to expect the student to demonstrate understanding in a more complete and objective way than he or she recognizes. The learner should show you prior writing assignments so the two of you can figure out the teacher's expectations.

Many teachers are finding increasingly useful ways for learners to develop and practice their writing, such as writing letters to dignitaries, ordering materials in the mail, producing newsletters, and contributing to literary magazines. At present, however, most school writing assignments are targeted toward a teacher who already knows what a student thinks and feels about particular issues. Talk often with your learners about what is expected and encourage them to ask the teacher many questions so they clearly understand his or her expectations.

Writing Stories

When learners are assigned to write narrative text—that is, a story—it can be helpful for them to know something about how stories are constructed. Before initial brainstorming about the topic and story elements, you may want to start by bringing up different examples of stories and talking about how authors vary in the way they construct their stories.

For instance, stories generally have a setting, characters, a problem, attempts to solve the problem, and resolutions to these attempts. The setting may be in the present, future, past, or once upon a time. Characters may be real or imaginary people, animals, or even aliens. Problems may be serious or humorous, with one

Science fiction:
An imaginary story based on current or projected scientific and technological developments.

Fable:
A short tale that teaches a lesson, often using animals and inanimate objects as characters.

Folk tale:
A story of unknown origin but well known in a particular culture through repeated telling.

Fairy tale:
A story about real-life problems, usually involving imaginary characters and magical events.

Realistic fiction:
Imaginative but believable narrative writing designed to entertain.

Nonfiction:
Text written using factual, real-life situations.

Myth:
A story passed down through oral tradition which explains natural phenomena, religion, or history of a race.

Mystery:
A carefully plotted story which contains an unknown element that the reader tries to decipher.

or more attempts by a protagonist to resolve them. And, of course, the story can tell of a real-life or an imagined experience. It can be especially helpful to consider the ways in which different types of stories work: science fiction, fables, folk tales, fairy tales, realistic fiction or nonfiction, myths, or mysteries. You may wish to set up a story planning sheet for your learners so they will be sure to include each of the story components listed above as they plan their stories.

Many stories have been composed through considering and rewriting stories from different angles. You may wish to find several examples of a common fairy tale, such as the "Cinderella" stories. Talk with your learners about the authors' various approaches to these stories. You might encourage them to draft a new version of an old tale. Or they may wish to consider a favorite story and rewrite it from the perspective of another character or in another setting or time.

Writing Informative Text

Writing informative text—a book report, history essay, or science project, for example—requires a different tack. Often assignments that require the writing of exposition are developed to cause students to investigate and think about a particular set of ideas. Thus, you will want to help your learners think of a topic they do not mind researching. Then students may peruse texts, encyclopedias, or other library reference materials before they begin to get ideas outlined in a cluster.

Informative text can be especially difficult for learners to compose because much of their reading experience has been tied to stories. They may not have had many opportunities to read informative texts or essays. So, an early step in helping your learners write informative text is exposure to it, perhaps from the form of essays in news and sports magazines, newspaper articles, and encyclopedia articles. Talk with your learners about how such pieces are organized and what kind of information they contain. Discuss the best way to organize ideas for the assignment at hand. Then get started by brainstorming and clustering, as described earlier.

Schumm & Hinchman

Completing Larger Assignments

Many writing assignments are larger in scope, and more time is given for their completion. Learners may be asked to complete projects, reports, or term papers. These sorts of assignments require additional planning. You can help your learners develop a realistic long-range plan and complete it in a systematic and timely way.

Understanding the Assignment

Ask your learners to bring you any printed directions that have been circulated by the teacher. Remind your students to ask questions and take copious notes of oral directions. You might even arrange a discussion group among learners from the class to be sure you're all on the right track.

As you talk with your learners about the assignment, think of questions they could ask the teacher in order to clarify it. Is a certain kind of product expected? Will the final product be displayed in any way, such as in a science fair, open house, or classroom showcase? Are learners allowed to work together? Are parents or other adults, including tutors, allowed to help? How much? How long should the piece be? What type or number of outside information sources are to be used? When exactly is the project due? Will there be extensions? Should the project be typed or handwritten?

Developing a Time-Management Plan

You can help learners manage their time by developing a written plan or a "to do" list connected to a timeline. Students can use this list to schedule time to develop a topic, complete necessary research, decide on the best form, and organize, write, and revise the piece by the due date. Help your student judge whether the timeline is realistic, considering all the other commitments he or she may have. For some learners, it may be helpful to start with the due date and work backward to set up a schedule. You will want to help them learn to leave a bit of "wiggle room" for revisions in the plan as they become more informed about the topic and the task. Also, unpredicted events in life may interfere with the ability to get work done when planned. You should also help them estimate the amount of time required to complete each task.

During this initial planning stage, you will want to consider sharing the different approaches many of us take to complete long-term projects. Some of us have a natural ability to complete tasks in a systematic and timely fashion. Others of us procrastinate until the deadline looms—and some procrastination can be all right. Many of us work on our projects by thinking about topics, approaches, and tone while we walk around and do other things. This is perfectly appropriate, provided there is room in the schedule to do so and still meet deadlines.

As you talk with your learners about being both realistic and systematic, be certain the plans that evolve from your discussion are really theirs. If a learner doesn't understand the plan or consider it his or her own, it's not likely to be used.

Refer to the plan as work progresses. There is no need to nag. Rather, bring the plan up in a conference to check it over. See if it continues to be realistic, and help each learner revise it as appropriate.

Helping Learners with Projects

Discuss the assignment and the teacher's expectations and brainstorm and cluster to narrow a project topic to something appropriate in scope and focus. A paper on a topic such as "religion" may be perfectly narrow for a fourth grader, but for a high school student the same topic will produce literally hundreds of angles and avenues unless the topic is narrowed.

If outside research is required for the project, learners should have a systematic way of collecting data. If they are required to do library work, check to be sure they know how to use appropriate library resources. Arrange a visit to the school or public library if needed, and ask the librarian to demonstrate how to look up information by subject, author, or title using the card catalog and gather data from newspaper microfiche, encyclopedias, *Who's Who* biographical references, the

Reader's Guide to Periodical Literature, and other reference materials.

Demonstrate the use of index cards for recording bibliographic information and notes, and be certain your student knows how to make a complete bibliographic entry for later use in the reference section of the paper. Your learners should ask the teacher about format and information requirements. While most students in elementary school are simply asked to note author, title, publisher, place of publication, and date of publication, high school students may be asked to use a specific bibliographic format. Help your learners avoid the frustration of completing a successful library search, getting near the end of writing a good paper, and discovering that the bibliographic entries do not have all the information required by the teacher.

Index cards can also work well if your learners are collecting information for a class project. Your learners may wish to talk to local experts or search through tapes of television or radio shows. In any case, they will want to make complete bibliographic entries for their sources. They will also want to take notes on what the source says. In some cases, tape recording an interview may be appropriate, but students will still need to transcribe these notes for later use in writing the paper. Time for transcription should be built into the long-range plan.

Help learners organize notes into categories to match the original clustering by topic and subtopic. The task may be made very concrete simply by finding a large floor space and grouping index cards appropriately. Revise original categories as needed, and talk about the form and organization the final product might take. Write down the outline, either in the form of clusters or in more traditional outline form.

Help learners decide on the final form of their project. Common formats include term papers, posters, dioramas, models, three-dimensional maps, plays, and short stories. The chosen format should speak to the main point of what learners wish to share about what has been learned through research. For example, a series of short plays, or vignettes, may be most appropriate for sharing research about behaviors of individuals in certain settings, a short story may be the best way to share historical information, and a term paper may be the best way to share information about the study of a country's present conditions. Be certain the learners talk to the teacher about ideas for format. The more interaction with the teacher at this stage of the planning process, the more chance learners will have of producing a project that the teacher really wants to see.

Encourage learners to simply start to draft reports or projects. Be sure that learners leave time for trying several different approaches and organizations and for following these through to logical conclusions. They will also want to leave a few days between drafts and revisions so they can take a more objective view of the piece and its strengths and weaknesses.

Make certain the students have made arrangements to transport the projects. Taking large maps or scale models to school may require a bit of thought so they make it in one piece.

A Final Word

Nalini, Earle, and Janet will find that while the suggestions in this chapter are a good starting place, additional "tricks of the trade" will emerge as they continue to work with their learners. We encourage you to be creative. Be imaginative and explore realistic, workable ways to help learners with assigned work. We also encourage you to continue to look in other sources for additional procedures to add to your tutoring repertoire.

CHAPTER 5

Effective Literacy Assessment

Jeri Sarracino
Beth Ann Herrmann
Barbara W. Batdorf
Ellen C. Garfinkel

This chapter describes how you can use a holistic approach to assess your learners' developing literacy abilities. The first section explains authentic assessment. The second section describes how to create and use portfolios. The third section shows ways to use the information in your learners' portfolios to make effective instructional decisions.

Authentic Assessment

For many years, educational assessment has been dominated by formal standardized tests. You are probably familiar with two types of standardized tests from your own school experiences: those that indicate what a person can do relative to specific objectives and those that indicate how a person's performance compares with that of others (Harris & Sipay, 1984).

Standardized tests help us understand some aspects of literacy progress, but they do not provide ongoing, descriptive information about individual learners. Authentic assessment is suited to the literacy tutor in four ways (Paris & van Kraayenoord, 1992). First, it focuses on what you are doing in your tutoring sessions. Second, authentic assessment provides you with opportunities to collect evidence of learners' progress from many sources, including standardized tests. Third, authentic assessment promotes learning because it involves the learners. Finally, authentic assessment measures what you *and* your learners value.

Authentic literacy assessment is based on several assumptions about literacy learning (Valencia, McGinley & Pearson, 1990). First, literacy learning is a dynamic process that takes place continuously, and learners and tasks change with every new instructional situation. Authentic assessment accounts for these changes over time. Second, literacy learning is multidimensional. Authentic assessment includes multiple measures of all aspects of learning. Third, literacy learning is an interactive process. Authentic assessment allows teachers and learners to collaborate. Also, learners can make independent judgments about their own literacy abilities through their involvement with the assessment process. Fourth, as explained in Chapter 3, literacy learning involves the development of positive attitudes, the ability to comprehend and create text, and knowledge of how reading and writing work. Authentic assessment can provide insight into these areas of literacy development. Finally, literacy learning leads to practical uses of reading and writing to meet real-life needs. Authentic assessment is anchored in genuine tasks and purposes (Edelsky & Harman, 1988).

A portfolio approach is one form of authentic assessment that is particularly useful for literacy tutors. A portfolio is a collection of artifacts and information about individual learners that is collaboratively selected by the tutor and the learners (Tierney, Carter & Desai, 1991; Valencia, 1990). A portfolio provides a holistic view of learners' literacy progress on an ongoing basis, which can help you make important instructional decisions.

What Does a Portfolio Look Like?
Portfolios come in many shapes and sizes and contain information characterized by four types of measures: formal measures, informal measures, process measures,

Sarracino, Herrmann, Batdorf, & Garfinkel

and product measures (Enoki, 1992). Each of these measures is explained in the following sections.

Formal Measures

As a literacy tutor you might have access to formal information about your learners. This information might include report card grades, standardized test scores, and the results of other school-like performance measures. Check with the director of your tutoring program about the availability of this type of information. It can provide you with an idea of your learners' literacy strengths and weaknesses, but, remember, it is only part of the whole picture.

Informal Measures

Informal information is descriptive. It can provide you with insight into your learners' literacy development that formal information does not. Informal measures are particularly useful in determining how well individual learners have met instructional goals set at the beginning of the learning period. It provides continuous information about learners' progress and helps you monitor knowledge about your learners' needs. Three types of informal measures are described as follows.

Checklists

A checklist can be used to systematically record information at any time, but it is particularly useful during observations. Most literacy tutors find that checklists can be completed fairly quickly and are easy to use. You will want to experiment with creating your own checklists. One interesting activity is for you and your learners to independently complete the same list. Then discuss both interpretations of their literacy progress. Two examples of checklists follow.

Mechanics and Usage Checklist

This checklist (Sharp, 1989) can be used to monitor specific qualities of learners' writing over time.

Learner's name _____

	Date_____			Date_____			Date_____		
	C	DC	NE	C	DC	NE	C	DC	NE
Writing Quality									
• self-selects topics									
• uses expansive vocabulary									
• uses complete sentences									
• uses complex sentences									
• uses revision strategies									
Writing Mechanics									
• has good handwriting									
• uses capitalization									
• uses lower case									
• uses periods									
• uses commas									
• uses quotation marks									
• uses exclamation points									
• uses correct grammar									

Key: C = Control, DC = Developing Control, NE = No Evidence

Comments and recommendations:

Checklist for Assessing Attitudes and Reading Habits

Learner's name _____ Date_____

Discuss the following items with the learner and record as much information as possible.

1. Do you read every word in a piece of reading material no matter what it is?
2. Do you read everything at the same speed?
3. When you read to yourself, have you ever noticed that you move your lips?
4. Do you tend to avoid reading something if you can get the information in another manner?
5. Do you feel it necessary to read most things over more than once?
6. Do you skip graphs, charts, pictures, or diagrams in reading material?
7. Do you *often* read a page of reading material and then realize that you really do not know what you have read?
8. Do you believe that you must *never* skip any portion of an article in a magazine or a chapter of a book?
9. Do you read any newspaper, magazine, or journal on a regular basis?
10. Do you believe that understanding what you read is more important than how fast you read?
11. Can you remember the main point or the plot of the last book you read?
12. Do you believe that people with large vocabularies are better readers than people with limited vocabularies?

Questionnaires

A questionnaire is a self-reporting instrument for assessing typical behavior or gaining useful information through questions. Questionnaires are especially useful in combination with observations. They can tell you about changes in your learners' attitudes toward reading and writing, abilities to comprehend and create text, and understandings about how reading and writing work. You can use the following Learner Concept Questionnaire (recommended by authors Herrmann & Sarracino, 1991) to explore changes in your learners' understandings about how reading and writing work.

Learner Concept Questionnaire

Learner's name _____ Date_____

Form completed by _____

Ask learners to look at a chapter in a content area book and answer the following questions.

1. Now that you have looked over the chapter, you can see that it is a textbook. Do you do anything differently to read a book like this as opposed to a story you are reading as a library book?
2. Do you do anything before you read a book like this? If so, what?
3. What would you do if you came up against a hard word?
4. What would you do if you didn't understand what you were reading?
5. What would you do when you finished reading this chapter?

The following Parent Concept Questionnaire (developed by Herrmann & Sarracino, 1991) can provide you with information from the learners' parents about how well they understand their role in their children's developing literacy.

Parent Concept Questionnaire

Learner's name _____ Date_____

1. Describe yourself as a reader.
2. What kinds of things does your child see you read at home?
3. How much do you read for fun at home? Please explain.
4. What things do you do at home to help your child become a better reader?
5. How confident are you that the things you are doing are helping your child become a better reader? Please explain.
6. How important are you in your child's literacy development?

The following Post-Lesson Questionnaire (recommended by Herrmann & Sarracino, 1991) explores changes in the learners' understandings of reading as a strategic reasoning process.

Post-Lesson Questionnaire

Learner's name _____ Date_____

Form completed by _____

1. What was your teacher teaching you today?
2. Why is it important?
3. When will you use it?
4. If you were showing someone else how to do this, what would you tell them to do?
5. How will what you learned today help you become a better reader or writer?

Finally, the following Enthusiasm Measure (adapted from McKenna & Kear, 1990) explores changes in learners' attitudes toward reading. The form was created by modifying an elementary reading attitude survey developed by McKenna and Kear (1990).

Enthusiasm Measure

Learner's name _____ Date_____

1. I enjoy my reading lessons.

Always   Sometimes   Never

2. Reading is interesting.

Always   Sometimes   Never

3. Reading is my best subject in school.

Always   Sometimes   Never

4. I care about reading better.

Always   Sometimes   Never

Sarracino, Herrmann, Batdorf, & Garfinkel

5. I like to read in front of people.

Always   Sometimes   Never

6. I like to read about new ideas.

Always   Sometimes   Never

7. I try hard to understand new material when I read.

Always   Sometimes   Never

8. I really like to read at home.

Always   Sometimes   Never

9. As I learn new ways to think about reading, I am more interested in reading.

Always   Sometimes   Never

10. I enjoy answering questions about stories I read.

Always   Sometimes   Never

11. I learn a lot when I read.

Always   Sometimes   Never

12. I like to read hard books.

Always   Sometimes   Never

13. I like to read aloud.

Always   Sometimes   Never

14. When I read hard books, I feel smart.

Always   Sometimes   Never

15. Reading is easy for me.

Always   Sometimes   Never

16. When I read about new ideas, I feel smart.

Always   Sometimes   Never

17. I can tell other people about the books I read.

Always   Sometimes   Never

18. I like to understand the important ideas when I read.

Always   Sometimes   Never

19. Learning new ways to think about reading makes me like reading more.

Always   Sometimes   Never

20. When I figure out difficult words or ideas in a story, I feel smart.

Always   Sometimes   Never

21. It is easy for me to answer questions about stories I read.

Always   Sometimes   Never

22. I think I read well.

Always   Sometimes   Never

23. I like to tell other people about books I read.

Always   Sometimes   Never

24. Reading at home is something I do well.

Always   Sometimes   Never

25. I can read harder books than I used to.

Always   Sometimes   Never

26. No matter how hard I try, reading either makes sense or it doesn't.

Always   Sometimes   Never

27. The best part of school is reading.

Always   Sometimes   Never

28. I feel like I am learning to be a better reader.

Always   Sometimes   Never

29. It is easy for me to understand the important ideas when I read.

Always   Sometimes   Never

30. My parents are pleased with my reading.

Always   Sometimes   Never

31. I like to figure out difficult words or ideas in a story.

Always   Sometimes   Never

32. I am good at reading.

Always   Sometimes   Never

33. I like to read because I learn a lot.

Always   Sometimes   Never

34. I like to read at home.

Always   Sometimes   Never

Learner self-evaluation is an informal assessment strategy that reveals what learners think of their own progress. Learners' responses to self-evaluation questions can provide a basis for discussion in conferences. Some examples of questions used in self-evaluations follow:

- What have I learned that I did not know before?
- What are my current strengths?
- What do I need to know more about?
- What are my goals for my next literacy activity?

Learners can respond to these kinds of self-evaluation questions orally or by writing in their journals. Such questions also provide a starting point for small-group discussions among learners. A sample Self-Evaluation Questionnaire (reprinted from Faigley, Cherry, Jolliffe, & Skinner, 1985) for writing follows.

Self-Evaluation Questionnaire

Learner's name _____ Date_____

1. List the most successful things you did in writing this paper.

2. List the things that a reader will think are successful.

3. List the things you were unable to do in this paper that would have made it more successful.

4. In the process of writing this paper, what aspects were easier than when you have written previous papers?

5. In the process of writing this paper, what aspects were more difficult than when you have written previous papers?

Interest inventories

An interest inventory is a questionnaire that explores an individual's strength and direction of interests. For example, an interest inventory can tell you about reading preferences, work and play interests, radio and TV habits, and other individual learner interests. You can develop more motivating instructional activities for your learners by knowing their interests. An example of an interest inventory (reprinted from Boning & Boning, 1957) follows. The items are adapted from an earlier version by Ruth Strang.

Interest Inventory

Learner's name _____ Date_____

1. Today I feel _____ .
2. When I have to read, I_____ .
3. I get angry when _____ .
4. To be grown up _____ .
5. My idea of a good time is _____ .
6. I wish my parents knew _____ .
7. School is _____ .
8. I can't understand why _____ .
9. I feel bad when _____ .
10. I wish teachers _____ .
11. I wish my mother _____ .
12. Going to college _____ .
13. To me, books _____ .
14. People think I _____ .
15. I like to read about _____ .
16. On weekends I _____ .
17. I'd rather read than _____ .
18. To me, homework _____ .
19. I hope I'll never _____ .
20. I wish people wouldn't_____ .
21. When I finish high school_____ .
22. I'm afraid_____ .
23. Comic books_____ .
24. When I take my report card home_____ .
25. I am at my best when_____ .
26. Most brothers and sisters _____ .
27. I don't know how _____ .
28. When I read math _____ .
29. I feel proud when _____ .
30. The future looks _____ .
31. I wish my father _____ .
32. I like to read when_____ .
33. I would like to be _____ .
34. For me, studying _____ .
35. I often worry about _____ .
36. I wish I could_____ .
37. Reading science _____ .
38. I look forward to _____ .
39. I wish _____ .
40. I'd read more if _____ .
41. When I read out loud _____ .
42. My only regret _____ .

Process Measures

Process measures provide evidence of how well learners are processing information. The following four types of process measures are useful for literacy tutors.

Observations and reflections

Ongoing, systematic observation of literacy learners is useful for two reasons. First, it helps you monitor the development of learners' attitudes toward reading and writing, their abilities to comprehend and create text, and their abilities to understand how reading and writing work. Second, it helps you revise and modify instructional goals to meet individual learner needs.

Learners' attitudes toward reading and writing are reflected in how they approach instructional tasks. Ask yourself these questions as you observe your learners confronting new tasks: Are they eager, or do they seem reluctant? Do they take risks by trying to read and spell unknown words, or do they timidly wait to be told? Do they view reading and writing as useful and functional tools? Do they value the role of reading and writing in their lives? Do they use reading and writing to meet everyday, real-life needs? Note how these traits change during and across lessons.

You can determine how well learners understand the content of what they read by observing and listening to their discussions. Use these questions as a guide to post-reading observations: Do they seem to have a good grasp of what they have read? If not, where did the breakdown in comprehension occur? How do the learners react when they realize they have misunderstood? Does their interpretation of text make sense?

You can observe the strategies learners use during reading and writing to determine how well they understand how the conventions of these activities work. Ask yourself these questions as you observe your learners during reading and writing tasks: What do they do when first encountering text? Do they just open a book and read? Or do they make use of the subtitles and pictures to orient themselves to the subject? While reading, do they self-correct misread words, or do they continue reading? When they come to a word they do not know, what do they do to figure it out? Are they using effective strategies? Initial observation of learners' strategies can provide the basis for effective decisions about which strategies to teach. After instruction, ongoing observations during reading and writing tasks can help you monitor learners' developing abilities with new strategies. This cycle of observation, reflection, and instruction can be used throughout the tutoring period.

Information obtained through observations should be recorded soon after it is obtained. Anecdotal records will help you keep track of information you gather through observations. These are ongoing, prose evaluations that describe each learner relative to his or her attitudes, strengths, needs, and literacy growth. An excerpt from a simple anecdotal record form (Sharp, 1989) follows.

Anecdotal Record

Learner's name _____ Date_____

Remarks_____

_____

_____

_____

_____

_____

You can use anecdotal records in your tutoring program to create a running account of incidents, observations, parent and learner comments, and other important notes. Information can be recorded immediately after it is observed or mentioned. It can later provide supportive evidence of changes in how the learners were thinking about reading and writing, the parents' roles in their children's developing literacy, and the learners' literacy abilities and attitudes toward reading and writing.

There are a number of ways to record anecdotal information. One way is to carry a clipboard at all times, recording observations and comments on a sheet of notebook paper which you can later transfer to anecdotal record forms. Another way is to record information on notecards that you can later tape or staple to individual record sheets. You may even want to record information on strips of adhesive mailing labels which you can later stick onto individual record sheets (Routman, 1991). Some general guidelines for observations and reflections follow (reprinted from Mathews, Young & Giles, 1992).

Observation Guidelines

Behaviors to observe during silent reading time

- How students select appropriate reading materials
- Length of time to select reading material each day
- Observations of students' behavior during the selection process
- Disputes over a particular book
- Are there "favorite" books in your group?
- Does the student read silently, read orally, look at pictures, not read, stare into space, disturb members of the group, or try to talk during reading?
- Does the student continue reading the same book or magazine each day?
- What behaviors are observed that seem to influence attentiveness?

Behaviors to observe during conferencing

- Is the student willing to share?
- Does the student try to monopolize the group, or does he or she say only what is minimal to participate?
- Do certain students conference better with each other?
- How do other members of the group react to the member sharing?

Behaviors to observe during prewriting and drafting stages

- How does the student choose a topic to write about?
- How does the student react to the freedom of self-selecting a topic?
- Does he or she use prewriting activities?
- Describe what the student does prior to writing a draft.
- Is it difficult to elicit oral discussion about the topic?
- During the writing of a draft, does the student write quickly, slowly, or painfully?
- How do you know that?

Behaviors to observe during writing conferences

- Is the student willing to share the draft?
- Does he or she self-edit?
- Is he or she satisfied with first draft?
- What comments help the student revise for meaning?
- Is the student willing to revise? How do you know this?

Behaviors to observe during volunteer- or teacher-directed activities

- Does student stay on task? What are the behaviors observed during teacher-manipulated activities?
- Does the student resume work on an ongoing project or assignment without prodding? Explain.
- How do members of group interact during required tasks?

Sarracino, Herrmann, Batdorf, & Garfinkel

Interviews

You can often explore what students are learning through interviews. These are especially useful when combined with observations. For example, you might observe that a student is hesitant to approach reading tasks and interpret that as fear of failure. The only way to know for sure is to ask. By interviewing learners, it is also possible to gain useful information about their attitudes and interests. Are they hopeful about being able to learn to read, or are they discouraged? What interests them most? This type of information will help you select materials and make instructional decisions.

Another reason for interviewing learners is to discover what they are thinking as they read. For instance, a learner might self-correct a misread word. In addition to noting that behavior, it would be important to know what the learner was thinking at the time. You can gain additional information about learners' reading abilities by asking them to verbalize their thought processes, such as having them explain how they knew they had misread a word.

Finally, parent interviews are useful for obtaining information about school-age children and their family histories relative to literacy learning. You may want to conduct an hour-long interview with each learner's parent to learn about the parents' educational backgrounds and literacy development and the role of *their* parents in their literacy development. The interviews should be conducted toward the middle of the semester—allow ample time first to build trusting relationships with the parents so they will feel comfortable discussing personal family information. You can ask parents to talk freely about their own school experiences, how they learned to read, and their parents' involvement in their developing literacy. You should conduct the interview as a conversation rather than a structured question and answer session, and it may be better to take notes rather than tape record these interviews to make parents feel even more comfortable. Be sure to check with the director of your literacy program before conducting parent interviews.

Retelling activities

Retelling activities can be useful for exploring the extent to which learners understand what they read. A Schema for Scoring Retellings (adapted from Mitchell & Irwin, 1990) follows.

A Schema for Scoring Retellings: The Retelling Profile

Directions: Indicate with a checkmark the extent to which the reader's retelling includes or provides evidence of the following:

	None	Low Degree	Moderate Degree	High Degree
1. Retelling includes information directly stated in text.				
2. Retelling includes information inferred directly or indirectly from text.				
3. Retelling includes what is important to remember from the text.				
4. Retelling provides relevant content and concepts.				
5. Retelling indicates reader's attempt to connect background knowledge to text information.				
6. Retelling indicates reader's attempt to make summary statements or generalizations based on text that can be applied to the real world.				
7. Retelling indicates highly individualistic and creative impressions of or reactions to the text.				
8. Retelling indicates the reader's affective involvement with the text.				
9. Retelling demonstrates appropriate use of language (vocabulary, sentence structure, language conventions).				
10. Retelling indicates reader's ability to organize or compose the retelling.				
11. Retelling demonstrates the reader's sense of audience or purpose.				
12. Retelling indicates the reader's control of the mechanics of speaking or writing.				

Interpretation: Items 1-4 indicate the reader's comprehension of textual information; items 5-8 indicate metacognitive awareness, strategy use, and involvement with text; items 9-12 indicate facility with language and language development.

Sarracino, Herrmann, Batdorf, & Garfinkel

You can use the Response to Literature Task that follows to explore changes in your learners' comprehension abilities and their knowledge of story elements. The form was based on a response to literature task developed by Au, Scheu, Kawakami, and Herman (1990).

Response to Literature Task

Learner's name _____ Date_____

Form completed by _____

Part I: Understanding the Story Frame

Directions: Ask the learner to read a story that presents a problem situation. Discuss the story with the learner. Mark the items that the learner discusses in sufficient detail.

- Characters   _____
- Setting   _____
- Problem   _____
- Events   _____
- Solution   _____
- Theme   _____
- Application   _____
- Personal Response   _____

Part II: Story Summary

Directions: Record the student's responses to the following questions:

- What is the problem in the story?
- How is the problem solved?
- What happened at the end of the story?

Conversations and conferences

Informal conversations with learners will provide you with valuable information about learners' thought processes during reading and writing. Conversations such as these help you build on learners' strengths and increase their repertoire of strategies. To illustrate this point, consider the following excerpt.

> Tutor: I see that you skipped the word "pillow" and then came back to it. Can you tell me what you were thinking that made you realize the word was "pillow"?
>
> Learner: Well, because I saw that the word started with a p and looked at the picture, and it was a pillow.
>
> Tutor: So, you used what the word started with and the picture to figure it out?

Learner: Yeah.

Tutor: Those are good strategies to use. I use them, too, but sometimes there aren't any pictures, so here's another one that I use. I read the rest of the sentence to see what's happening. For instance, in this story, the little girl picked up something on her bed to look under for money, so I would see that and then think about what I find money under after I lose a tooth. It's my pillow, so I would figure she would find money under her pillow, too. Making connections from my life to what is happening in the story is another strategy to use to figure out words I don't know.

Ongoing conversations such as these are helpful throughout the entire period of instruction for informing both you and your learners what has been learned and what is yet to be learned about useful reading and writing.

It is also revealing to talk to learners about the content of what they have read. This will help you know whether the learners have understood what they have read and how they are using their prior knowledge to comprehend text. Rather than assuming learners have misunderstood something, it is beneficial to ask them why they think as they do. Their reasoning may come directly from their experiences rather than being a case of misunderstanding. For instance, after reading a story about a person who is always helping others, a learner may say that the character is motivated by selfishness. This response may seem unusual, but questioning the learner may reveal that a certain person in the learner's life has always helped others but only for reasons of personal gain. In this way, you would realize that your learner was making connections to real life experiences, which is considered to be a useful reading strategy.

Likewise, regularly scheduled conferences are also a good way of assessing learners' writing progress. They will help you develop a better understanding of attitudes as well as abilities. Writing conferences should focus on questions such as: Do you understand why language conventions are important? How do you know when something needs to be changed? What do you see as your strengths, and what needs more work? What is your best piece? Why? What goals would you like to set for yourself as a writer?

Experiment with your own ways to conduct conversations and conferences with your learners. You might find the following conference guidelines (developed by Kathy Hinchman of Syracuse University in New York) helpful at the beginning of your tutoring program.

Conference Guidelines

- Start with some background questions.
  (a) What brought you to this class?
  (b) What did you like about school? What didn't you like?
  (c) What is your current employment or volunteer interest?
  (d) Is reading or writing very important to your job or other parts of your life?
  (e) What other kinds of job or education would you like to be involved in?

- Are you involved in learning anything new right now? (Give examples)

- What do you like to read? (Example: novels, newspaper [ad sections, letters to the editor], church hymns, bulletins) What would you like to read better?

- Do you talk about what you have read with other people? How?

- What do you do when you are reading and come to something you don't know?

- Who is a good reader that you know? What makes that person a good reader?

- What do you like to write? (Example: letters, shopping lists, phone lists) What would you like to write better? Do you share your writing with others?

- Who is a good writer that you know? What makes that person a good writer?

- What would you like to be able to do when you finish this program that you cannot do now? Explain.

Guidelines and suggestions for conducting writing conferences (reprinted from Mathews, Young & Giles, 1992) follow.

Guidelines and Suggestions for Conducting Writing Conferences

Guidelines for tutors when conferencing with a learner:

- Respect the writer's integrity as a writer.
- Be tactful!
- Give lots of encouragement.
- Find something good about the paper and express it to the writer.
- Emphasize meaning as the most important element of writing.

Comments to make after the learner has read his or her writing to you:

- I understand you to be saying _____.
- I understand your main point to be _____.
- What I like about this piece is _____.
- I would like to know more about _____.

Questions to help writers read their works for content and clarity:

- Do you like what you have written? What part do you like best?
- Does it say what you want it to say?
- Did you include everything you wanted to say?
- Does it make sense to you?
- Is each new idea presented in logical order?

Product Measures

You and your learners will want to collaboratively select a few finished products to include in their portfolios. Finished products help you and your learners explore attitude and knowledge changes over time. Several types of products can be included, but be selective—more does not necessarily mean better in this case.

Three-dimensional materials

Learners can include three-dimensional materials in their portfolios to demonstrate literacy growth and change. They might include creative materials such as art, video and audio tape recordings, and recorded presentations. Have fun experimenting with other three-dimensional materials that demonstrate learning.

Sarracino, Herrmann, Batdorf, & Garfinkel

Writing samples

A good way to determine learners' progress is to examine written work on an ongoing basis. Try using an individual writing folder to store each learner's writing throughout the tutoring period, from rough drafts to final edited copies.

As you review rough drafts you may want to use the following guide for examining written work (developed by Beth Ann Herrmann).

A Guide for Examining Written Work

1. Is the writing becoming more complex?
2. Are understandings of language conventions improving?
   - spelling
   - usage
   - punctuation
   - capitalization
   - sentence and paragraph sense
   - sentence and paragraph structure
   - overall organization
3. Is the writing becoming clearer?
   - ideas focus on a topic
   - content is appropriate
   - word usage is appropriate
   - message is clearly presented
4. Is ability to edit own work improving?
5. Are sources for writing ideas expanding?
   - from the imagination
   - from discussion with others
   - from books, stories, poems, or a television show
   - from the teacher
6. Are forms of writing produced becoming more varied?
   - narrative writing
   - poems
   - persuasive writing
   - expository writing
7. Are writing topics becoming more varied?
   - topics about which the writer is an expert
   - topics learned before writing
   - topics about things in the past, present, or future
   - topics about abstract ideas
8. Are writing audiences becoming more varied?
   - teacher
   - classmates
   - people known
   - people unknown
9. Is fluency (length) improving?
10. Is writing becoming more enjoyable?

Journals

Two types of journals are particularly useful for assessing learners' progress on an ongoing basis. First, personal journals allow learners to experiment with different types of entries. They may wish to write a reaction to what they have read, or they may write about how it relates to their lives. They may choose to write a character analysis, or they may simply summarize what they have read.

Second, dialogue journals provide learners with opportunities to use writing for real-life communication purposes. In these journals, learners write back and forth to you or each other about things they have read. The learners can write the same kinds of entries they would in a personal journal, but the difference is that someone actually responds to what they have written. It is best if the respondents are the same throughout the tutoring period so there is a consistent, ongoing conversation about what is being read. An example excerpt from a dialogue journal follows.

> Learner: Dear Ms. Jones. I really liked the story we read today about Amelia Earhart. She was a fascinating person. What do you think happened to her? Michelle.
>
> Tutor: Dear Michelle, I'm glad you liked reading Amelia Earhart's story. She is a good role model for adventuresome young ladies like yourself. I think she is still out there "flying" somewhere, don't you?

See Chapter 1 for more information on dialogue journals.

Logs

A log is a record of an activity or process. An example of an activity log follows.

Activity Log

Learner's name _____   Date_____

	Activity	*[Time]*
Monday		
Tuesday		
Wednesday		
Thursday		
Friday		
Saturday		
Sunday		

You could use this log with your learners' parents to obtain information about the kinds of at-home literacy activities the parents and their children are participating in and the amount of time they spend on each activity. Each week you could ask parents to provide a brief description of reading or writing activities they have engaged in with their children each day and the amount of time spent on each. This information can be used to provide supportive evidence of how increased parent involvement helps their children's developing literacy. An activity log can also be used by adult learners to keep track of their at-home literacy activities.

Using Information to Make Decisions about Instruction

Information generated by a portfolio approach can help you plan instruction and make decisions about appropriate instructional materials. The Progress Report that follows can help you organize your thoughts about learners' reading and writing growth and progress.

Progress Report

Learner's name _____ Date _____

Person completing this form _____

Reading

1. What changes and/or improvements have been made in the learner's:
   * attitude toward self and reading?
   * ability to comprehend text?
   * understandings about how reading works?
2. Strengths
3. Weaknesses
4. Recommendations

Writing

1. What changes and/or improvements have been made in the learner's:
   * attitude toward self and writing?
   * ability to create cohesive text?
   * understandings about how writing works?
2. Strengths
3. Weaknesses
4. Recommendations

Ask each of your learners to complete the same form to evaluate their own progress. Then compare and discuss your completed report with learners.

You should be able to identify your learners' strengths and needs from the information collected in anecdotal records, questionnaires, conversations, writing, and conferences. You may have noticed some learners struggling with vocabulary acquisition. You may have seen that others were having trouble editing their writing. After addressing these needs, you may observe other areas that need attention. This cycle of assess-teach-assess will help you keep up with individual needs throughout the tutoring period.

Authentic assessment will also help you identify your learners' interests. It is much easier to improve literacy abilities if you use materials that capture and hold students' interest. Through conversations, conferences, and interest inventories you will be able to identify their major areas of interest.

Based on what you learn about your learners' strengths, needs, and interests, you can select appropriate materials. For instance, if you know that a learner's strengths include using context clues to figure out unknown words, you will not have to worry about choosing books with a completely familiar vocabulary. On the other hand, if reading from context is a strategy that a learner lacks, the choice of reading material would be different. If a person's job requires following written directions, you could help by providing practice with how-to manuals. It is important to use a variety of materials that will both support your learners with what they already know and challenge them to learn more.

Reluctant readers can be enticed to read with materials that interest them. Some readers prefer stories, while others find the newspaper interesting. Still others might respond to historical material. From the information gleaned from the assessments you have done, you will know what types of materials to have on hand for your learners.

A Final Word

Authentic assessment can provide you with valuable information about your learners. In this chapter, we have provided you with practical tips and suggestions for using one form of authentic assessment—a portfolio approach. Feel free to modify any of the forms or techniques we have suggested to better meet the needs of your learners. You will also want to experiment with creating your own forms and techniques.

References

Au, K.H., Scheu, J.A., Kawakami, A.J., & Herman, P.A. (1990). Assessment and accountability in a whole literacy curriculum. *The Reading Teacher, 43*(8), 574-578.

Boning, T., & Boning, R. (1957). I'd rather read than.... *The Reading Teacher, 10,* 197.

Edelsky, C., & Harman, S. (1988). One more critique of reading tests—with two differences. *English Education, 20*(3), 157-171.

Enoki, D.Y. (1992, April). Student portfolio and profiles: A holistic approach to multiple assessment in whole language classrooms. Paper presented at the meeting of the American Educational Research Association, San Francisco, CA.

Faigley, L., Cherry, R.D., Jolliffe, D.A., & Skinner, A.M. (1985). Assessing writers' knowledge and processes of composing. Norwood, NJ: Ablex.

Harris, A.J., & Sipay, E.R. (1984). *How to increase reading ability: A guide to developmental and remedial methods*. White Plains, NY: Longman.

Herrmann, B.A., & Sarracino, J. (1991, April). Improving student literacy through parent involvement. Paper presented at the annual meeting of the American Educational Research Association, Chicago, IL.

Mathews, S.R., Young, J., & Giles, N. (1992). *Student literacy volunteers: Providing "tools" for brighter futures*. Pensacola, FL: The University of West Florida.

McCaig, R.A. (1981). A district-wide plan for the evaluation of student writing. In S. Haley-James (Ed.), *Perspectives on writing in grades 1-8*. National Council of Teachers of English.

McKenna, M.C., & Kear, D.J. (1990). Measuring attitude toward reading: A new tool for teachers. *The Reading Teacher, 43*(9), 626-639.

Mitchell, J.N., & Irwin, P.A. (1990, December). Analyzing text and text-related recalls. Paper presented at the National Reading Conference, Miami, FL.

Paris, S.G., Lawton, T.A., Turner, J.C., & Roth, J.L. (1991). A developmental perspective on standardized achievement testing. *Educational Researcher, 20*, 12-20.

Paris, S.G., & van Kraayenoord, C. (1992). New directions in assessing students' reading. *Psychological Test Bulletin, 5*(1), 20-26.

Routman, R. (1991). *Invitations: Changing as teachers and learners K-12*. Portsmouth, NH: Heinemann.

Sharp, Q.Q. (1989). *Evaluation: Whole language checklists for evaluating your children*. New York: Scholastic.

Temple, C., & Gillet, J.W. (1989). *Language arts: Learning processes and teaching practices*. New York: HarperCollins.

Tierney, R.J., Carter, M.A., & Desai, L.E. (1991). *Portfolio assessment in the reading-writing classroom*. Norwood, MA: Christopher-Gordon.

Valencia, S.W., (1990). A portfolio approach to classroom reading assessment: The whys, whats, and hows. *The Reading Teacher, 43*(4), 338-340.

Valencia, S.W., McGinley, W., & Pearson, P.D. (1990). Assessing reading and writing. In G.G. Duffy (Ed.), *Reading in the middle school*. Newark, DE: International Reading Association.

CHAPTER 6

Where to Go When You Need More Help

Bird B. Stasz
Bob Schlagal

Up to now this book has covered how to tutor adults and children and those in between. We have discussed how to construct a meaningful lesson and the importance of helping learners develop positive self-esteem. We have included information on language, how it works, and its relationship to reading. The authors have even provided some instructional and assessment strategies and activities to get you started.

The time will come, if it hasn't already, when you will be out the door and into a classroom or library to tutor for real. Picture this: you are sitting down to tutor—maybe this is your third or fourth session—and suddenly you realize that what you really need is more "stuff." You may need more good books to use with children or adults. You may need some resources to give you pointers on special reading and writing needs. You may need additional strategies for writing and story analysis. The question is: where do you find more sources, more ideas, and extra help to meet the needs of your learners? The purpose of this chapter is to help you move beyond this book so you can find additional material easily.

One of the first places to look for answers to more technical questions is in the references at the end of the chapters in this book. These references are useful in and of themselves, but they also help you get a foothold on a particular area of interest. Much of the work cited represents original work in the field and can give you a fine head start in the long journey of additional reading.

Another good source of information is educational journals. We have included an annotated list of journals, compiled by Regie Routman (1991), just to get you started. Many of them probably will not appear in your public library, but you can find many of them in the library at your local university or in a school district or superintendent's office. Journals like *The Reading Teacher* are available with an annual subscription membership to the International Reading Association. This is a large professional organization, and many teachers are members. You can always ask around to see who has the journals and borrow them. You can also get them through your public library on interlibrary loan.

Finding articles on specific topics becomes a matter of being a good research detective. Many libraries have large indexes such as the *Education Index* that list titles of articles by topic. There are also many computer databases available, such as ERIC. The limiting factor is the type of library available in your area. If you live in an urban area or near a college, your chances of doing journal research are greater than if you live in a small rural community with a small library.

Good books for children are not as hard to find as one might think. There are lots of lists of "best" books available. The Association of Library Service to Children of the American Library Association publishes a list of "Best Children's Books" every year. The young adult service of the American Library Association also publishes a "Best Young Adult List." The Caldecott and Newbery Award winners lists, available from your local library, also are a wonderful source of books for children. Finally, don't be afraid to use yourself as a source of good books for kids. Think back to your own early reading days. Other people will probably enjoy the books you treasured. You might even want to try writing your own children's stories.

Finding good materials for adults is harder. We have included a short list of high interest-low readability materials. However, the best low-level materials are those created by the learners themselves. These are commonly known as Learner Generated Material (LGM). The advantage to using these kinds of books in tutoring sessions is that they are about things your learners can relate to and are written by other "new" readers.

Another source of material for adults is what we call "real stuff"— that is, magazine articles, newspaper clippings, stories, and poems that can be found in many publications. As a general rule, most newspapers are written at about the sixth grade level. The key ingredient in selecting material for adults is interest. You will find that your learners are infinitely more successful at improving their reading and writing abilities if you allow them to select books, topics, or magazines. Finally, we have included a short volunteer checklist at the end of this chapter to help you get started and to answer some of the most commonly asked questions.

Educational Journals

Democracy and Education
   4 issues per year/subscription $12
   The Institute for Democracy and Education
   College of Education
   119 McCracken Hall
   Ohio University
   Athens, OH 45701-2979

   A quality journal written by and for teachers that focuses on issues related to democratic practice. For example, recent themed issues have addressed tracking and ability grouping, democratic management, and alternatives to standardized testing.

Educational Leadership
   8 issues per year/subscription $32
   Association for Supervision and Curriculum Development
   1250 North Pitt Street
   Alexandria, VA 22314-1403

A journal for elementary, middle school, and secondary teachers and administrators interested in being on the cutting edge of current educational theory and practice. For anyone interested in being well informed about good ideas regarding today's educational practices.

Elementary School Journal
5 issues per year / subscription $45 (institutions); $28.50 (individual); $19.50 (students)
University of Chicago Press
5720 South Woodlawn
PO Box 37005
Chicago, IL 60637

Geared toward a more scholarly audience, this journal contains studies, research reviews, and analyses of ideas for elementary teachers, administrators, teacher educators, and researchers.

English Journal
8 issues per year / subscription $35
(includes membership in NCTE)
National Council of Teachers of English
1111 Kenyon Road
Urbana, IL 61801

By teachers for teachers in middle, junior, or senior high school, *English Journal* contains quality, thought-provoking articles about theory, practice, and new ideas in learning, reading, and writing in the classroom.

The Horn Book Magazine
6 issues per year / subscription $36
14 Beacon Street
Boston, MA 02108

For anyone interested in quality writing for children and young adults, *The Horn Book* provides the most complete, responsible, and thoughtful coverage. Contains announcements of forthcoming titles; reviews of children's and young adult literature, poetry, and nonfiction; biographies; articles from authors about their work; and articles on using literature in the classroom.

Journal of Reading

8 issues per year / subscription $38
International Reading Association
800 Barksdale Road
PO Box 8139
Newark, DE 19714-8139

Peer-reviewed articles on research, theory, and practice for those interested in teaching reading at middle school, junior high, high school, college, and adult levels. Material may be geared toward a more academic audience. Regular departments present information on young adult literature, current issues in reading, middle school teaching, classroom materials, and research summaries. April issue is guest and themed.

Language Arts

8 issues per year / subscription $35
National Council of Teachers of English
1111 Kenyon Road
Urbana, IL 61801

Theory and practice in language learning are combined with exceptional literary style in monthly themed journals. This official journal of NCTE (for the elementary grades) notes its new publications, forthcoming conferences, and reviews of children's and professional books.

Learning

9 issues per year / subscription $18
Springhouse Corporation
1111 Bethlehem Pike
Springhouse, PA 19477 (correspondence)
PO Box 2580
Boulder, CO 80322 (subscriptions)

This lively journal contains creative suggestions from teachers for teachers, practical applications for the classroom, activities, tips, and a reader exchange. For those interested in teaching K-8. Teachers new to the field should be aware that articles cover a broad spectrum from traditional to whole language approaches.

The New Advocate
4 issues per year/subscription $28
PO Box 809
Needham Heights, MA 02194-0006

Noted authors, illustrators, and educators share their perspectives on children's literature and related issues in this outstanding literary journal. Book and media reviews are included.

Phi Delta Kappan
10 issues per year/subscription $30
Eighth & Union
PO Box 789
Bloomington, IN 47402

Concerned with issues relating to leadership, research, trends and policy, *Phi Delta Kappan* (named for the educational fraternity) is a must for those truly interested in what's happening in our schools today. Contains an annual Gallup poll of this country's attitude toward public schools.

The Reading Teacher
8 issues per year/subscription $38
International Reading Association
800 Barksdale Road
PO Box 8139
Newark, DE 19714-8139

This practical journal for preschool and elementary teachers focuses on teaching approaches and techniques and also includes reviews of children's books. Departments deal with reading around the world, professional development, reading assessment, integrating curriculum, issues and trends, and the U.S. National Research Center. Subscription includes *Reading Today*, a bimonthly newspaper about the profession.

Young Children
6 issues per year/subscription $30

National Association for the Education of Young Children
1834 Connecticut Avenue Northwest
Washington, DC 20009-5786

Preschool and early elementary teachers will find this journal to be thought provoking, informative, and supportive in the area of professional growth. Major issues and ideas in the field are discussed. Contains such items as a calendar of conferences, book reviews, Washington updates, and a section of reader commentary.

Professional Resources for Working with Young Children

Duffy, G., Roehler, L., & Herrmann, B.A. (1988). Modeling mental processes helps poor readers become strategic readers. *The Reading Teacher, 41,* 762-769.

The authors describe and illustrate the modeling and practice of comprehension strategies. The emphasis is on making sound practices in comprehension "visible" to learners so that these may be practiced and perfected.

Green, F. (1988). Listening to children read: The empathetic process. *The Reading Teacher, 39,* 538-543.

Green describes a method for listening to children read in a non-threatening way. He gives guidance as to the types of oral reading errors that may be usefully ignored and those which should result in teacher queries, specific modeling, or correction.

Monson, D. (Ed.). (1985). *Adventuring with books: A booklist for pre-K–grade 6.* Urbana, IL: National Council of Teachers of English.

This popular resource is a broad-ranging annotated bibliography of quality books for kids. The entries are organized by age/grade, theme, and genre (such as folktale, fantasy, picture book, and so forth).

Nessel, D., & Jones, M. (1981). *The language experience approach to reading: A handbook for teachers.* New York: Teachers College Press.

This is a very solid and readable book. It addresses elementary level reading, writing, and thinking skills. It is especially strong at the primary grades and easily adaptable to tutoring conditions.

Radencich, M.C., & Schumm, J.S. (1988). *How to help your child with homework.* Minneapolis, MN: Free Spirit Publications.

This is an especially good resource for volunteer tutors who are trying to help their charges keep up with their work or catch up from being somewhat behind. It supplies a variety of approaches to developing good study habits and the basics of supporting learners. Often the demands on tutors do not go far beyond the guidelines and techniques presented here.

Slavin, R.E. (1984). Students motivating students to excel: Cooperative task and student achievement. *The Elementary School Journal, 85,* 53-64.

Slavin reviews the research on cooperative learning and student achievement, describes typical cooperative structures, and accounts for the positive results in terms of differing incentives. Group tasks that reward individual achievement via group rewards appear to affect motivation and achievement most profoundly.

Stauffer, R.G. (1970). *The language-experience approach to the teaching of reading.* New York: Harper & Row.

This is an excellent and comprehensive book on the teaching of reading. It is readable, useable by tutors, and richly deserves its classic status. In this book, Stauffer covers important procedures in reading instruction using dictated stories, creative writing, word banks, and a strategy-based comprehension approach.

Teale, W.H. (1982). Toward a theory of how children learn to read and write naturally. *Language Arts, 59,* 555-570.

In this piece, Teale makes the case that reading and writing can be learned naturally and supports it from several points of view. It is basically a position piece and serves to orient readers to the holistic view of literacy learning.

Professional Resources for Working with Adults

Davidson, J.L., & Wheat, T.E. (1989). Successful literacy experiences for adult illiterates. *Journal of Reading, 32,* 342-347.

Outlines using a modified seven strand Language Experience Approach for working with adults.

Forester, A.S. (1988). Learning to read and write at 28. *Journal of Reading, 31,* 604-613.

Comparison of literacy acquisition between adults and children. The article suggests that when learners are at the "information center" positive learning takes place.

Kirby, D., & Liner, T. (1981). *Inside out development strategies for teaching writing.* Montclair, NJ: Boynton/Cook.

This is a lively, interesting text that outlines a process-oriented developmental writing program. The exercises can be used in a one-on-one tutorial situation but are more effectively used in small groups.

Macrorie, K. (1984). *Searching writing: A context book.* Montclair, NJ: Boynton/Cook.

Macrorie is one of the pioneers in process writing. This book introduces the idea of I-search papers, which holds the student's interests and life in the center of the research process. Good exercises and easy to use.

Mosenthal, P.B., & Kirsch, I.S. (1989). Designing effective adult literacy programs. *Poetics, 18,* 239-259.

The authors present a technical and research perspective of desiging adult literacy programs. The paper discusses a set of "psychological design criteria" that should be considered when designing a literacy program. The article is useful if you are interested in the research underpinnings of the field of adult literacy.

Olson, G. (1983). *Sweet Agony II: A writing book of sorts.* Medford, OR: Windyridge Press.

This is a very light-hearted and useful little book on the mechanics of writing and publishing. It would be appropriate in a learner-generated publishing workshop.

Ponsot, M., & Deen, R. (1982). *Beat not the poor desk.* Portsmouth, NH: Boynton/Cook.

Great ideas for developmental writing classes. The greatest strength of the text is that it shows the reader how to move from the "parable" to the essay.

Stasz, B.B., Schwartz, R., & Weeden, J. (1991). Writing our lives: A basic skills program. *Journal of Reading, 35,* 30-33.

The article outlines a writing program for Head Start moms using their own experiences.

Stasz, B.B., & Adams, M. (1993). *Telling stories writing lives: A handbook for adult beginning writers.* New York: Cambridge/Regents Press.

This book is part of a GED writing series. Oral history methodology and lots of flexible writing examples give students opportunites to practice writing for the essay section of the GED exam.

Young, D., & Irwin, M. (1988). Integrating computers into adult literacy programs. *Journal of Reading, 31,* 648-652.

The article describes ways in which word processors can be used in adult literacy programs. All the suggestions have been field tested in an adult education project in Eastern Maryland.

General References

Calkins, L.M. (1986). *The art of teaching writing.* Portsmouth, NH: Heinemann.

This is one of the "must read" books in process writing with elementary school children. Calkins outlines how to do writing workshops with school children.

Harman, S., & Edelsky, C. (1989). The risks of whole language literacy: Alienation and connection. *Language Arts, 66*(4), 392-406.

Harman and Edelsky outline some of the "life" consequences of using the whole language approach. There is a politics of change that is important to consider when using bottom-up learner centered curriculum with adults.

Harman, D. (1987). *Illiteracy: A national dilemma.* New York: Cambridge Press.

This is a short and very user-friendly book that outlines some of the major themes and problems in the ongoing adult literacy discussion.

Kozol, J. (1985). *Illiterate America.* New York: Doubleday.

This is a fiery and impassioned look at illiteracy in America. Kozol is not always logical or accurate, but he writes with amazing power and conviction. If you ever thought that literacy was not a problem in the United States, this book will convince you otherwise.

Gillet, J.W. & Temple, C. (1993). *Understanding reading problems.* New York: HarperCollins.

This is a solid and readable text for the person who wants to know a lot about the reading problems of young children.

Raphael, T., & Englert, C. (1990). Writing and reading: Partners in constructing meaning. *The Reading Teacher, 43*, 388-400.

Cognitive strategy instruction in writing that improves elementary school children's writing.

Strubel, A. (1992). *Multicultural resource list.* For a copy write to: Student Coalition for Action in Literacy

Education (SCALE), Education Department, University of North Carolina-Chapel Hill, Campus Box 3500, Chapel Hill, NC 27599

SCALE is a nonprofit literacy organization that promotes literacy volunteerism on college campuses nationwide. Their materials are uniformly excellent. This resource list is no exception. Packed with annotations, book lists, and contact people in institutions, it is a useful and concise presentation of a variety of materials for tutors.

Sources for High Interest-Low Readability Materials

Benefic Press
1900 North Naragansett
Chicago, IL 60639

Continental Press, Inc.
520 East Bainbridge Street
Elizabeth, PA 17022-9989

Cornerstone Books/
  Monthly Review Press
122 W. 27th Street
New York, NY 10001
212-691-2555

Crestwood House/
  Macmillan
866 Third Avenue
New York, NY 10022
800-257-5755

EMC
300 York Avenue
St. Paul, MN 55101
800-328-1452

Globe-Fearon
P.O. Box 2649
Columbus, OH 43216
800-848-9500

High Noon Books/
  Academic Therapy
  Publications
20 Commercial Boulevard
Novato, CA 94949-6191

Jamestown Publishers
Box 9168
Providence, RI 02904
800-USA-READ

Pendulum Press, Inc.
Academic Building
Saw Mill Road
West Haven, CT 06516

Raintree Steck-Vaughn
P.O. Box 26015
Austin, TX 78755
800-531-5015

SRA/Macmillan/McGraw Hill
P.O. Box 543
Blackwick, OH 43004
800-843-8855

Sprint, Action, Double
  Action/Scholastic
P.O. Box 7502
Jefferson City, MO 65102
800-325-6149

Yearling Books, Robot
  Series/Dell Publishing
1540 Broadway
New York, NY 10036
800-223-6834

The toll-free telephone numbers listed may not be accessible world-wide.

Assessment Resources

The resources in this section focus on the holistic approach to evaluation and question the usefulness of standardized testing. We would like to see more portfolio and alternative assessment procedures used in schools. However, it should be noted that standardized tests are not all bad. They do tell you something about a student—if only that there is sometimes a discrepancy between a child's test performance and what you believe to be true about that student's academic performance. The resources suggest that you maintain a slightly critical eye when it comes to assessment in general.

Barrs, Myra; Ellis, Sue; Tester, Hilary; & Thomas, Anne. (1989). *The primary language record: Handbook for teachers.* Portsmouth, NH: Heinemann.

Baskwill, Jane, & Whitman, Paulette. (1988). *Evaluation: Whole language, whole child.* New York: Scholastic.

Clay, Marie M. (1985). *The early detection of reading difficulties (3rd ed.).* Portsmouth, NH: Heinemann.

Cohen, S. Alan. (1988). TESTS: *Marked for life.* Richmond Hill, Ont.: Scholastic-TAB.

Goodman, Kenneth S., Goodman, Yetta M., & Hood, Wendy J. (Eds.). (1989). *The whole language evaluation book.* Portsmouth, NH: Heinemann.

Harp, Bill (Ed.). (1991). *Assessment and evaluation in whole language programs.* Norwood, MA: Christopher-Gordon.

Jett-Simpson, Mary (Ed.). (1990). *Toward an ecological assessment of reading progress.* Schofield, WI: Wisconsin State Reading Association.

Kamii, Constance (Ed.). (1990). *Achievement testing in the early grades: The games grownups play.* Washington, DC: National Association for the Education of Young Children.

Tierney, Robert J., Carter, Mark A., & Desai, Laura E. (1991). *Portfolios in the reading-writing classroom.* Norwood, MA: Christopher-Gordon.

Ammon, Richard. (1988, Fall). Evaluation in the holistic reading/language arts curriculum. In *Oregon English theme: Whole language.* Portland, OR: Oregon Council of Teachers of English (pp. 65-69). (An earlier version first appeared in Hardt, Ulrich, (ed.). (1983). *Teaching reading with the other language arts.* Newark, DE: International Reading Association.)

This article looks at holistic evaluation and specific strategies and ideas for evaluation of the language arts. The article includes excellent reflective questions for the teacher.

Au, Kathryn H., Scheu, Judith A., Kawakami, Alice J., & Herman, Patricia A. (1990, April). Assessment and accountability in a whole literacy curriculum. *The Reading Teacher, 43,* 574-578.

Based on their work in the Kamehameha Elementary Education Program (KEEP) in Hawaii, the authors address teachers' concerns about assessment and accountability with a "whole literacy" approach. They recommend a portfolio approach that incorporates a curriculum framework based on six aspects of literacy. They also suggest five major assessment tasks for providing information on the six aspects of literacy. Specific examples of assessment tasks are provided.

Bailey, Janis, Brazee, Phyllis, & others. (1988, April). Problem solving our way to alternative evaluation procedures, *Language Arts, 65,* pp. 364-373.

A group of teachers describe their attempts to move toward evaluation that is consistent with their meaning-centered approaches to reading and writing. This is a terrific article, both for understanding holistic evaluation and for the literacy evaluation forms and checklists that are shared.

Brandt, Ronald (Executive Ed.). (1989, April). *Educational leadership: Redirecting assessment.* Alexandria, VA: Association for Supervision and Curriculum Development.

Don't miss this comprehensive, provocative, and outstanding issue for perspectives on the current state of assessment and for directions for meaningful assessment.

Bredekamp, Sue, & Shepard, Lorrie. (1989, March). How best to protect children from inappropriate school expectations, practices, and policies, *Young Children, 44,* 14-24.

Assessment and standardized testing is a reality in all public schools. This article challenges the use and misuse of test scores as they direct and redirect a child's education.

Cambourne, Brian, & Turbill, Jan. (1990, January). Assessment in whole language classrooms: Theory into practice. *The Elementary School Journal, 90,* 337-349.

This article makes a solid case for the validity of responsive evaluation.

Eggleton, Jill. (1990). *Whole language evaluation, reading, writing and spelling.* Bothell, WA: The Wright Group.

This is a hands-on guide to help teachers and tutors evaluate children's early or emerging literacy efforts.

Fisher, Bobbi. (1989, November/December). Assessing emergent and initial readers. *Teaching K-8,* 56-58.

A real-life kindergarten teacher suggests ways to systematically observe, record, and assess children's work.

Harman, Susan. (1989-1990). The tests: Trivial or toxic? *Teachers Networking: The Whole Language Newsletter,* Vol. 9, no. 1, pp. 1, 5-9.

Harman reflects on the damage done to children's educational experience by standardized testing. She further suggests that teachers' professional judgment in evaluating students should be relied on more than it is.

Harp, Bill. (1988, November). When the principal asks: 'When you do whole language instruction, how will you keep track of reading and writing skills?' *The Reading Teacher, 42,* 160-161.

The author answers the rhetorical question posed in the title by giving specific examples of how to develop a holistic evaluation of children.

Hornsby, David, & Sukarna, Deborah, with Jo-Ann Parry. (1988). Record keeping and evaluation. In *Read on: A conference approach to reading.* (pp. 129-143). Portsmouth, NH: Heinemann.

Similar to the above article, the authors offer practical suggestions for holistic evaluation.

Johnston, Peter. (1987, April). Teachers and evaluation experts. *The Reading Teacher, 40,* 744-748.

The author supports the general belief in whole language classrooms that standardized testing is not useful in furthering instruction. He also suggests that teachers' observations and interactions with students play a much larger role in the evaluation procedure.

King, Dorothy F. (1989-1990). My word! Real kids or unreal tasks: The obvious choice. *Teachers Networking: The Whole Language Newsletter,* Vol. 9, no. 1, pp. 14-15.

This article is about a teacher's worst fear, getting back low standardized test scores in an interactive whole language classroom.

Koskinen, Patricia S., Gambrell, Linda B., Kapinus, Barbara A., & Heathington, Betty S. (1988, May). Retelling: A strategy for enhancing students' reading comprehension. *The Reading Teacher, 41,* 892-897.

The authors focus on the idea of retelling and its uses in the classroom.

Neill, D. Monty, & Medina, Noe J. (1989, May). Standardized testing: Harmful to educational health. *Phi Delta Kappan, 70,* 688-697.

Multiple choice tests come under question in this article because their results drive school placements for children. Further, the author suggests that multiple choice tests encourage the teaching of isolated, discrete basic skills rather than critical and integrated thinking.

Reardon, S. Jeanne. (1990, Winter). Putting reading tests in their place. *The New Advocate*, 29-37.

A primary teacher suggests that children should be taught to test read and that this specific skill will help them perform better on standardized tests.

Rogers, Vincent. (1989, May). Assessing the curriculum experienced by children. *Phi Delta Kappan, 70*, 714-717.

The author suggests that students need a different kind of assessment to determine what they have learned in content area courses. He offers a variety of activities that could become part of any alternative assessment program.

Seidel, Steve. (1989, December 13). Even before portfolios: The activities and atmosphere of a portfolio classroom. *Portfolio: The Newsletter of Arts Propel*, pp. 6-9.

Seidel deals with the ins and outs of using portfolios in a 9th grade classroom.

Sharp, Quality Quinn (Compiler). (1989). *Evaluation: Whole language checklists for evaluating your children.* For grades K-6. New York: Scholastic.

This is a small book of checklists that are useful in helping teachers and tutors evaluate students in the whole language classroom.

Teale, William H. (1988, November). Developmentally appropriate assessment of reading and writing in the early childhood classroom. *The Elementary School Journal, 89*, 173-183.

This article provides a theoretical basis for using alternative assessment methods such as observation and performance samples for young children.

Valencia, Sheila. (1990, January). Assessment: A portfolio approach to classroom reading assessment: The whys, whats, and hows. *The Reading Teacher, 43*, 338-340.

Another article on the how-to's of portfolio assessment.

Watson, Dorothy (Ed.). (1987). Valuing and evaluating the learners and their language. In *Ideas and insights: Language arts in the elementary school* (pp. 209-219). Urbana, IL: National Council of Teachers of English.

Watson offers another practical article on strategies for alternative assessment procedures.

Weaver, Constance. (1988). How can we assess readers' strengths and begin to determine their instructional needs? In *Reading process and practice: From socio-psycholinguistics to whole language* (pp. 321-363). Portsmouth, NH: Heinemann.

The best part of this article is the guidelines for miscue analysis.

Wiggins, Grant. (1989, April). Teaching to the (authentic) test. *Educational Leadership, 46*, 41-47.

Wiggins offers a radical departure from standardized assessment at the secondary school level by suggesting the development and use of "skills of inquiry."

Wolfe, Dennie Palmer. (1989, April). Portfolio assessment: Sampling student work. *Educational Leadership, 46*, 35-39.

The author suggests that school assessment needs to be more closely aligned to real life and that students need to be involved in long-term projects that require integrated cross-disciplinary thinking.

Wood, George (Coordinator). (1990, Fall). *Democracy in education: Alternatives to standardized testing.*

This is a discussion starter for anyone interested in the issue of standardized testing versus alternative assessment.

Volunteer Checklist

References aside, the reality is that at some point you are going into your site as a volunteer. The suggestions that follow are simply advice about things we think are important. This is a minimal list and is meant only as a guide to help you get started.

1. Introduce yourself early!

Call ahead to your site and make an appointment with your "supervisor" or contact person before you volunteer. It is important to meet the people you will be working with before your volunteer obligations begin.

2. Do your homework!

Learn as much about the organization or institution where you are volunteering as you can before you begin. It is helpful to read any brochures they may have and be familiar with the mission statement if there is one. Try to learn about the clientele of the organization so you know whom and what to expect.

3. Be prepared for anything!

Make up an "emergency activity bag" that you can carry with you when you go to volunteer. Sometimes a volunteer will be asked to improvise in a situation without much prior instruction. Therefore, it is good to have materials and activities that allow you to think fast on your feet. Try to select materials and make up packets of activities that can cover a wide variety of situations, such as an individual setting or small group work. Also, make sure the activity you create does not require specialized or prior knowledge.

4. Keep a secret!

The relationship between tutor and learner demands a high level of confidentiality. Tutors become the personal educators of many students. In that role, volunteers find themselves in the sometimes uncomfortable position of learning more about their clients than they would like to know. Everything a client tells you must be held in the strictest confidence *except* when you suspect abuse, neglect, unlawful acts, or you believe the student's well being is threatened. This is especially true if the student is a minor.

5. Get connected!

Always try to establish a personal connection with the folks that you tutor. That connection can be anything from people you both know to foods you both like to experiences you have shared.

6. Be careful, your biases are showing!

Tutoring in any situation demands a great deal of sensitivity to issues of class, gender, and cultural perspective. What is nifty for you in your culture may be revolting to someone else who sees the world through different eyes. By the same token, what you think of as everyday could be totally extraordinary to someone else. In your tutoring try to use learning examples that are common to most people. Keep in mind that your mission is to help folks learn—not to offend or impress.

7. Be clear!

It is important that everyone in the tutoring situation understands "the edges of the envelope." Make sure you understand the expectations of the organization and supervisor and that you transmit those expectations clearly to the learner. For example, if the student is working toward a GED, you need to be knowledgeable about what that entails. If a student has specific goals, make sure you know what they are and can work with the student to help him or her achieve those goals.

8. Learning is a partnership!

Remember that learning is a partnership. You need to model the same behaviors and skills you want your students to have. Your tutoring is most successful when you and the learner work together. Rarely do people learn much when they feel they have little part in the process.

9. Be positive and have fun!

Folks need to feel good about themselves and about what they are doing. It is impossible to be too positive or have too much fun. Try to be upbeat and optimistic even if you are feeling otherwise.

10. Be committed!

Volunteer tutoring is a very special undertaking. Folks will grow to depend on you. They will stop you in the supermarket to say hello and introduce you to their relatives. Keep your commitments, be on time, and let them know far in advance if you are not coming for some reason.

Some Final Thoughts about Literacy and Tutoring

Bird B. Stasz

You have come to the end of our practical guide for tutoring—for organizing the general nuts and bolts of a supplemental reading and writing program for children and adults. By now you are undoubtedly well saturated with information about tutoring and are ready to go out into the field and do it. You probably have your site all picked out, have met the people you are going to be working with, and maybe even have met your learners. The first couple of lessons are ready to roll. If you are like most tutors, you spend a fair amount of time and energy in activities, such as cutting out paper pumpkins until midnight to augment that perfect vocabulary game for the first graders or reading endless short stories to find that perfect fit for your first day in the adult basic education classroom. Now I invite you to sit back and relax, just for a few moments, and reflect on some final thoughts about literacy: its power, its limitations, its magic, and its place in the world.

Many politicians and government officials love literacy and, by extension, love illiteracy. It gives them something to talk and write about that, at least on the outside, looks as benign as apple pie. Literacy and illiteracy in all their many forms are the subject of campaign speeches and political promises. There is an underlying assumption on the part of these politicians that everyone knows and agrees on what literacy is and is not. Usually illiteracy is something to be "stamped out" rather like a brush fire or seen as an easily curable disease—take a dose of tutoring and call me in the morning. Folks who don't read and write well are seen as lacking in some way. They are operating from a position of weakness rather than strength. If only they could "get literacy" they would be up to par with everyone else and all would be well. Literacy in the political and educational context is invested with a peculiar kind of power. To "have literacy" is somehow to be better, more clever, and more productive in a societal sense. The more literate we are as a society the better able we are to compete successfully in the international economic arena. There are lots of figures on how much illiteracy "costs" different countries. Literacy, then, becomes all wound up with the gross national product, economics, and social productivity.

Research suggests that literacy is, at best, a very slippery concept. Literacy looks different depending on where the term is applied and by whom. For example, literacy in the Alaskan bush does not look the same as it does in New York City (Stasz & Eringhaus, 1988). Likewise, there is a literacy of coastal Maine fishermen that is distinctly different from the literacy of rural papaya growers in Hawaii. Further, literacy is not entirely defined by the industrialized West. In some parts of the world, literacy is associated with use. Perhaps the language of conversation is not the same as the language of print, such as in Arabic. Or consider the Vai of Northern Liberia who use their native language to carry on conversations and personal correspondence, Arabic to read and interpret the Koran, and English to carry out the formal business of government and commerce (Scribner & Cole, 1981). There are all different kinds of literacies, each one with a unique flavor and set of parameters. In large measure, depending on where you are on the globe, literacy becomes a question of culture and society.

For example, in our program, one particularly talented tutor came to my office perplexed. She had been immersed in a sociology course with a dynamic professor who introduced her to the works of Paulo Freire, a Brazilian educator who espouses political transformation through literacy. She got all fired up and became the driving force behind a community-based literacy program for pregnant teenagers and young mothers. On one occasion she asked one of her students why she was trying to learn to read better. Instead of the idealistic response she anticipated, the young woman said, "You learn to read so you can be a typist." The fact that this statement could be translated as "You learn to read so you can have a job and a job makes you somebody" is not entirely obvious to someone who already is somebody. My point here is that it often happens that you view literacy through one set of lenses and your student through another. However, it is this exchanging of lenses that makes literacy tutoring such a powerful experience for everybody involved. Such is the power of communication.

On a grand scale, the acquisition of literacy skills will not cure the social ills of a complex industrialized society, and it will not eliminate poverty or discrimination or cure cancer. It is not a vaccine that will instantly protect and improve the health and well-being of individuals who are inoculated. The reality is that there are lots of people who cannot read and write and who live wonderfully warm, productive lives.

What literacy is—and herein lies its power—is a configuration of skills that, taken collectively and offered in a nurturing, holistic, and creative way, can provide individuals with a new lens for looking at the world. Under the right circumstances literacy tutoring can give voice to those who have been silent by providing opportunities. In a sense, literacy tutoring can chronicle and preserve the past, as in the stories of one generation told for another; it can ease the lines of difference and promote opportunities for inclusion. The power of literacy, then, does not lie in the rhetoric of politicians and in the needs of corporations, but in the language that illuminates the landscapes and lives of people.

The magic of literacy exists in the magic of stories. Stories are the glue that hold a culture together, the thread that connects the saint to the sinner, the banker to the gypsy, the great novelist to the six-year-old. Stories give us a common language and a moral imagination. They are our access to a collective past and our glimpse of the future. Stories extend across generations and through time. Stories present us with heroes and heroines: plain people doing extraordinary things.

Everyone has stories and everyone knows stories. It is part of the magic of being a literacy tutor that you can help people find their voices and record their reminiscences. The reading, writing, and publishing of stories validate and legitimize the experiences of learners who for many reasons have stayed in the shadows of our culture. Stories allow you to explore those issues that are central to the lives of your learners. Robert Coles (1989) suggests that literacy practitioners must be careful in what they say to learners because "their story, yours, mine—it's all we carry with us on this trip we take, and we owe it to each other to respect our stories and learn from them" (p. 30).

Finally, literacy occupies a peculiar place in our world. On the one hand, it is seen by many in the Western world as the panacea for every social ill going; on the other hand, it is just one more academic hoop. Some folks jump through it and some folks don't. In reality, despite the best efforts of the political and educational system, literacy is as important to the folks you are tutoring as they want to make it. They will decide where reading and writing fit into their lives. As a tutor you are in the unique position of being able to offer the opportunity to be heard and the opportunity of access. Literacy tutoring is heady stuff; you will learn far more than you will ever teach.

References

Coles, R. (1989). *The call of stories: Teaching and the moral imagination*. Boston, MA: Houghton Mifflin.

Scribner, S., & Cole, M. (1981). *The psychology of literacy*. Cambridge, MA: Harvard University Press.

Stasz, B.B., & Eringhaus, M. (1988). *Culture and the nature of literacy*. Paper presented at the International League for Social Commitment in Adult Education, Toronto, Ontario, Canada.

Author Index

Note: An "f" following a page number indicates that the reference may be found in a figure.

Subject Index

Note: An "f" following a page number indicates that the reference may be found in a figure.

book

PLAYS: 31; learner-devised, 75-76

PLOT, STORY: 31

POEMS: 31; journal review of, 106; learner-written (*see* Biopoems); newspaper/magazine, 105; as writing inspiration, 97. *See also* Personality Poems; Verse

PORTFOLIOS: 23, 116, 117, 120, 121; contents of, 96-99; defined, 78; instruction informed by, 99-101; types of, 78-99

POSTERBOARD: 17

POSTERS: 75; letter-sound, 39

POST-LESSON QUESTIONNAIRE: 82

PREDICTION, BY LITERACY LEARNERS: 21; encouragement of, 12-13; as Read Aloud element; 42; about stories (*see* Story Impression Strategy); test-related, 55, 57

PREPOSITIONS: 40

PRESCHOOLERS: and literacy, 16

PREWRITING: 90

PRINT: written language and, 18

PRIOR KNOWLEDGE: 18, 29-30, 44, 45; defined, 29; as Read Aloud resource, 42; as reading aid, 94; retelling and, 92. *See also* K-W-L approach

PROCESS MEASURES: 88-96

PROCESS WRITING: 111, 113

PROFILES, RETELLING. *See* Schema for Scoring Retellings

PROGRESS REPORTS: 99-100

PRONOUNS: 40

PRONUNCIATION: 42

PUBLICATION: of learner writing, 70, 112

PUNCTUATION: 40, 70, 97. *See also* Capitalization

Q

QUESTIONNAIRES: 81-82, 86-87, 100. *See also* Interest inventories

QUESTIONS: assessment-oriented, 88; avoiding personal, 5; calculated, 11-12; conversational, 93-94; implicit modeling–related, 25; during learner conferences, 94-95; oral reading–inspired, 109; practice pretest, 55, 57, 63-64; as Read Aloud element, 42; reading comprehension–related, 8; response to literature task–related, 93; self-evaluation, 86; as SQ3R element, 36; storybook-related, 16; for tutor use, 117. *See also* "Three Questions"

QUOTATION MARKS: 80

R

READ ALOUDS: 42

READER'S GUIDE TO PERIODICAL LITERATURE: 75

READING: 90; aloud (*see* Reading aloud); and comprehension, 8, 29; for enjoyment/entertainment, 28, 37; implicit modeling and, 25; for information, 37; and knowledge, 28-29; and language, 15; as lesson element, 8-9; for meaning, 20, 37, 117; mechanics of, 88-92; and mental modeling, 24; oral (*see* Reading aloud); and phonics, 25; in primary grades, 21; purposes of, 28, 36-37; reasoning and, 23, 44, 45; as SQ3R element, 36; success at, 27-46; thinking and, 44-45; writing and, 29. *See also* Choral reading; Fluency, reading; Language; Read Alouds; Repeated Readings; Rereading; Response to Literature Task; Retelling activities; Words

READING ALOUD: by learners, 9, 42, 109; to preschoolers, 16; by tutor, 9, 24, 42; as writing aid, 69. *See also* Read Alouds; Sounds

READING TEACHER, THE: 104, 108

READING TODAY: 108

REASONING: encouragement of, 12; and mental modeling, 24; reading and, 23, 44, 45; strategic, 23-24, 45; writing and, 23, 44, 45

RECITATION: as SQ3R element, 36. *See also* Retelling activities

RECORDS: literacy-tutor, 3. *See also* Anecdotal records

REPEATED READING: 41

REPETITION: student reliance on, 59

REPORT CARDS: tutor reference to learner, 79

REREADING: as Read Aloud element, 42

RESEARCH: tutor, 104 (*see also* Articles, professional—as tutor resource); writing-related, 72

RESOURCES: tutor, 3, 103-124. *See also* Dialogue journals; Portfolios

RESPONSE TO LITERATURE TASK: 93

RETELLING ACTIVITIES: 92-93; 119. *See also* Repeated Readings

REVIEW: as SQ3R element, 36

REVIEW SHEETS: student, 60, 61, 63

REVISION: by learner writers, 80, 90; of Read Aloud stories, 42; as writing essential, 66, 67, 68-69

REWARDS: lesson activity–related, 9

REWRITING: of existing stories, 72. *See also* Revision

RISKS: importance of literacy-related, 12-13

S

SALINGER, PIERRE: 55

SCAFFOLDING: 24

SCALE (Student Coalition for Action in Literacy Education): 114

SCHEMA FOR SCORING RETELLINGS: 92

SCHOOLS: literacy programs

in, 2

SCHUMM, JEANNE SHAY: 5, 42

SCHWA: 38

SCIENCE FAIRS: 73

SCIENCE FICTION: 72

SCIENCE PROJECTS: learner reports on, 72

SEIDEL, STEVE: 120

SELF-EVALUATION: learner, 86

SELF-EVALUATION QUESTIONNAIRE: 86

SEMANTICS: 25. *See also* Words

SEMANTIC WEBBING: 43

SENTENCES: 70, 80, 92, 97; clustering in, 68; sequencing of, 8; topic, 70; transition, 70. *See also* Paragraphs; Punctuation

SEQUELS: to Read Aloud stories, 42

SETTING, STORY: 31. *See also* Story Parts activities

SHIRLEY (Cox/Kreuger preschooler): 18

SHORT STORIES: learner-devised, 75-76

SHOWCASES: classroom, 73

SIGHT WORDS: 40, 41f

SILENT CONSONANTS: 38f

SLAVIN, R.E.: 110

SOFT (LETTER) SOUNDS: 38f

SOUNDS: language as, 16 (*see also* Pronunciation); letters and, 37-39. *See also* Blends; Digraphs; Diphthongs; Schwa

SPEAKING: as literacy element, 15. *See also* Language; Pronunciation; Words

SPELLING: 6, 97; risk-taking in, 88; as writing element, 70

SQ3R STRATEGY: 36

STANDARDIZED TESTS: 65, 105; critiques of, 116-121; domination of, 77; tutor reliance on results of, 79

STAUFFER, R.G.: 110

STORIES: 31; comparison of two, 33; construction of, 71; interpretation of (*see* Echo Reading; Personality Poems; Story Frames; Story Impression Strategy; Story Mapping; Story Parts activities; Venn Diagrams); learn-

er-written, 27, 71-72; magazine, 105; nature of, 71-72; rewriting, 72, sequencing (*see* Story Mapping, via circular pictures); of Shirley, 18; student revision of, 42; tutor-written, 104; value of, 127-128; as writing inspiration, 97. *See also* Fables; Fairy tales; Fiction; Folk tales; Mystery stories; Myths; Parables; Read Alouds; Short stories

STORYBOOKS: 21; as preschooler resource, 16

STORY FRAMES: 32

STORY IMPRESSION STRATEGY: 34

STORY MAPPING: 31; through circular pictures, 35

STORY PARTS ACTIVITIES: 33

STORY PYRAMIDS: 31

STRANG, RUTH: 86

STUDY: student approach to, 59

STUDY GUIDES: 60, 63

SUBHEADINGS: text, 70

SUBTITLES: as reader aid, 88

SYNTAX: 25. *See also* Sentences; Words

T

TAGGART, KAY: 17

TEACHERS: and literacy programs, 7, 48-51, 54, 56, 58, 60, 61, 90; as tutor coordinators, 3, 6, 66; and writing assignments, 66

TEALE, W.H.: 110

TELEVISION: as source of writing ideas, 97

TERM PAPERS: 73, 75-76

TESTS: essay, 65; inadequate, 58-59; multiple-choice (*see* Multiple-choice tests); standardized (*see* Standardized tests); tricks of taking, 64-65; true-false, 63, 65; tutors and learner, 54-65; value of, 116

TEXT. *See* Writing

TEXTBOOKS: tests based on, 56-57

THINKING: and implicit model-

ing, 25; language and, 15; and mental modeling, 24; reading and, 44-45; strategic, 25; writing and, 44-45. *See also* Reasoning

"THREE QUESTIONS" (game): 5

TIME: as critical test factor, 64-65

TOPICS, WRITING: 97

TRUST: as learner/tutor essential, 4-5, 10, 53, 122

TUTORING LOGS: 51

TUTORS, LITERACY. *See* Literacy tutors

U-V

UNDERSTANDING. *See* Comprehension

USAGE, ENGLISH: 40, 97

VAI: languages of, 126

VENN DIAGRAMS: 33

VERBAL REHEARSAL: 12

VERBS: 40

VERSE: 31

VIDEOTAPES: 33; class notes explained using, 58; as portfolio contents, 96

VOCABULARY: 80, 92, 101; building, 40, 41, 43

VOICED DIGRAPHS: 38f

VOICELESS DIGRAPHS: 38f

VOWEL DIGRAPHS: 38f

VOWELS: 38f. *See also* Diphthongs; Schwa

W

WATSON, DOROTHY: 121

WEBBING. *See* Semantic webbing

WHOLE LANGUAGE THEORY: 113, 119, 120

WHOLE LITERACY THEORY: 117

WHO'S WHO: 74

WIGGINS, GRANT: 121

WORD BANKS: 110

WORDS: connotations of, 18; implicit-modeling approach to unknown, 24-25; key, 34; Language Experience Approach focus on, 27; from letters, 37; meanings of, 43; misreading of, 88, 91; sight, 40, 41f; unfamiliar, 24-25, 42, 88-89, 101; writer choice of, 70. *See also* Grammar; Language; Letters (characters); Parts of speech; Phonics; Phrases; Pronunciation; Punctuation; Semantics; Sentences; Syntax; Usage; English; Vocabulary

WORKSHEETS: tutor assistance with, 53

WRITERS, PROFESSIONAL: 42, 69; articles by, 106-107; techniques of, 71

WRITING: assessment of learners', 97-99; comprehension and, 20; for enjoyment/ entertainment, 28, 31; expository, 31, 36, 97; free, 68; implicit modeling and, 25; informative, 72; and knowledge, 28-29; and language, 15; and meaning, 37, 117; mechanics of, 70-71, 88, 90, 92, 112; and mental modeling, 24; narrative, 31-35, 97 (*see also* Stories); nature of, 66, 67-69, 71; persuasive, 97; in primary grades, 21; reading and, 29; reasoning and, 23, 44, 45; structure of, 31-36; student, 8 (*see also* Dialogue journals); success at, 27-46; "to the teacher," 71; thinking and, 44-45; tutor assistance with assigned, 66-76; types of, 31; uses of, 28, 36-37. *See also* Essays; Fiction; Handwriting; Language; Letters (characters); Letters (correspondence); Literature; Paragraphs; Prewriting; Print, Process writing; Rewriting; Stories; Usage, English; Words

WRITING WORKSHOPS: 113

Y

YOUNG CHILDREN: 108-109